"In this year I remembered my own youth and it came together with my own age."

Kathryn Martin had raised her children and taught in public and private schools for twenty-seven years before she retired in 1965. She hoped that retirement would be a new adventure, but it turned out that instead of adventure she found depression increased by loneliness and a fear of old age.

In *A Question of Age* the author records her reckless plunge into the world of youth when in 1969 at the age of sixty-one she became "housemother" in a college dorm of forty-nine girls in a small New Hampshire college. Her essays on events and vignettes of individual students are filled with wry humor and insight. Her patience and endurance sustained her as well as many of these young women with whom she lived during those difficult days. She was recalled to her own youth, but more importantly she found in her work and associations a return to vitality and a reenforcement of her lifelong belief and support for the equality of opportunity for women.

Names have been changed (including that of the college), two years experience has been combined into one, and several of the individuals described are combinations of two or more actual students. Still, the story rings true, and women everywhere will find something to which to relate: college students, alumnae, those approaching or newly retired, educators, and perhaps psychologists.

A Question of Age

The Dorm and I

Naught cared this body in wind or weather
When youth and I lived in't together.

COLERIDGE, *Youth and Age*

A Question of Age

The Dorm and I

Kathryn Martin

TOMPSON & RUTTER

Grantham, New Hampshire

First published 1981 by

Tompson & Rutter Inc

Grantham, NH 03753

© Copyright 1981 by Kathryn Martin

All rights reserved

Manufactured in the United States of America

Library of Congress Cataloging in Publication Data

Martin, Kathryn
A question of age.

1. Martin, Kathryn.
2. Retirement—Psychological aspects.
3. Housemothers—New England—Biography.
4. Conflict of generations.
I. Title.

LA2317.M274A35   371.1′0092′4 [B]   80-27057
ISBN 0-936988-01-0

to Judy Child

ACKNOWLEDGMENTS

Grateful acknowledgment is made to Professor Richard Eberhart for permission to use his name and to include a description of his seminar at his home in Hanover, to all those in the class whose unpublished poems have been quoted in whole or in part, and to Dr. William Nolen for permission to quote briefly from his book *Healing*. Ten lines from "Shine, Perishing Republic," by Robinson Jeffers have been reprinted from *The Selected Poetry of Robinson Jeffers* (© 1925, renewed 1953 by Robinson Jeffers) by permission of Random House, Inc. Special thanks are due Dorothea Steil, for her excellent typing assistance and encourgement, and to my daughter, Alberta Keeney, for her enthusiasm and help.

Although this story is based upon a real experience, proper names of individuals have been changed (with one exception) as have most place names. Several characters in this book are composites, and two years' experience has been condensed into one.

I owe many thanks to the girls of Bixby dorm who were in the process of becoming women. They were radical only in their determination to reject what was irrelevant to their own growth, and were gentle with me when I tried to do the same. It was a true meeting so moving to me that I wrote this book, a partial record of many encounters.

Contents

SPRING

10

Prologue

"I don't want to die." This is the first sentence in *Healing* by Dr. William Nolen. There are ways of dying, and one is the psychological death which occurs when the patient quits in the midst of a life crisis, sinking into feelings of helplessness, living too much in the irrevocable past and unable to face the hazardous future.

During the time I spent in Bixby dorm at Wadleigh Junior College for Women, the most frequent comment I heard from old acquaintances was, "How do you stand it? I would go crazy." I had no ready answer, for I was unwilling to reveal the state of mind that had taken me there. I went to Wadleigh in the autumn of 1969. All that we heard of the college generation in that year filled me with apprehension: the riots, the bombings, the rejection of all our accustomed ways in favor of violence. Now that we remember our panic of terror and guilt when Cambodia and Vietnam fell, now that we have witnessed in Watergate the corruption of power, we can appreciate from a distance what happened in the minds of the young. They had mistrusted the government before we did, and this toppled their trust in the older generation and its material values of "success."

My personal distress was complicated. Now as I approach my seventy-second birthday, I wonder why I felt so old and used up at sixty. Was it merely that this signified to me the beginning of old age? I had retired from teaching in California, where I had spent my adult life teaching and writing and raising my own children who were then in their thirties; they were married and had their own children. I retired on a disability pension for rheumatoid arthritis, and in a state of emotional exhaustion. In 1967 I had a serious surgical operation.

I was the youngest member and the only daughter of my family, with three older brothers; my close connections with my original family were all ended—my parents and my three brothers were dead. A profound sense of loss followed these deaths; all these people had been a continuum in my life. The students were gone; my family was gone; my children, so long the center of my life after a failed marriage, were no longer children.

My first visit to New Hampshire had occurred in 1959, and thereafter I spent my summers in rural New England, two of them at the MacDowell Colony in Peterborough, New Hampshire, working on a book published in 1962. These were halcyon summers when the writing went well, and New Hampshire was a relief from the dry, hot summers of the West. I took a romantic view of the green and pleasant land; it seemed more like home than home, as if I were living in one of Jung's "archetypal memories" of my ancestors. When I retired, I wanted to return and find a new adventure; I did not fancy settling down among the old environs, glued to the past.

When I came to New Hampshire to live, I settled for the first year in a college town some distance from Wadleigh College, which I did not know existed. From my apartment windows in an old house, I could see the students going to and fro. They looked unkempt, dirty, and busy, but they provided a vicarious feeling of life less startling than what I had seen in Berkeley. I intended to write. One of the illusions about retirement is that we will have *time*; it is, however, often a shock to discover that we have too much time and too few encounters with the outside world. Or perhaps we do not wish to spend our time in social forays, shopping and chit-chat, in no true meeting, in repetitions.

The writing went badly. I viewed it with immense distaste; there was a sense of contriving. For a while I put this down to the irritability of the convalescent, but I knew at a deeper level that I did not really *care*. The writing retreated like a dog under the bed who would not be coaxed out, exactly as it had in the days when I neglected it because of the exigencies of my profession.

"You won't like the winters," everyone said. This was rather like New Yorkers who say they hate New York, but it was a change from Californians who assure one it is the greatest place on earth because of the climate, neglecting to mention that autumn is hot as hell and the winter rains can go on for months at a time. I was dazzled here by the fiery leaves and the frosty air of autumn; the first fall of snow came in the night and surprised me when I woke to a downy silence and a completely white landscape.

Then a sense of isolation began to grow like a fungus in my mind, and it continued to grow despite efforts to entertain new friends, or the generosity of old friends from the summers at MacDowell. I got through the winter with a visit to my children at Christmas, but the measure of my days was a creeping illness, *accidie*, so well described by W. H. Auden in *A Certain World*, "tedium or perturbation of the heart." For months into the spring I coped (how the busy brain deceives!) and visited doctors to find out if I were ill. "You are a prime candidate for a heart attack," one of them said.

When I was invited to take a trip to England in June, I jumped at the idea; this was an escape, a grateful time. My passport picture was more appalling than most; it showed me depleted to near zero, fragile, pale, blank. After I returned, the students had gone away for the summer, and the town seemed vacant of all life; it was not a town for tourists. I viewed life through a thin glass which deprived me of sensation; I was living in a peculiar lassitude, but "going back" was an intolerable thought. My life seemed a vacant stage where no action appeared; the play had bombed. I had an obstinate pride and a loss of energy that made moving my possessions a task too big to contemplate.

These are symptoms of depression. Even as I write this, I hate recalling the cover-up; the cheerful letters, the painful pleasantries, the guests I did not enjoy, the books I put down from weariness. There was a refusal to admit the loneliness that lay like a grey film over my emotions. I had been lonely before; I had learned to enjoy solitude. I would not admit the necessity of "social props" to one's self-esteem: a social status, a professional life, children I was proud of, family, old friends who knew me surrounded by all this.

Part of my despair that year is more clear to me now in view of the women's revolution of the past ten years, but at this time I had barely heard of "Women's Lib." My generation did not question that "The Seven Ages of Man" had nothing to say about women. The nineteenth century laid its dead hand on women of my generation by prescribing roles with rigid directions on how one played them: sister, daughter, wife, mother, teacher, even divorcee. The pedestaled goddess and the "fallen woman" were images implanted in the young feminine heart of my time. "The good woman," whose "price was above rubies," fulfilled her role, rubies or no. However well or poorly I enacted these roles assigned to me, (sometimes with several of them overlapping) I was never entirely myself in any of them, for they were founded on legends, on images, on woman's belief that she could survive only through an elaborate diplomacy. There was pain and disappointment when my nature, my own needs, caused disagreements with the people I loved. What they expected me to be was programmed. Certainly I was in collusion with all this until 1938, when my marriage fell apart and I returned to college to fulfill the boring task of "teacher training." The mold was broken, but the old roles remained with my relatives, who were loyal, if somewhat shocked at "the first divorce in our family." I heard with inner fury, "You are committing suicide . . . you are destroying your children's economic security . . . you are not strong enough to earn your living . . . Who will *entertain* you?"

14

They were wrong. I managed nicely, if unconventionally; but by age sixty, only the grandmother role remained, and I was by no means ready to settle for playing it full time. I was at the end of my emotional rope, still clinging there to the Micawberish hope that something would turn up.

By August on the day of my sixty-first birthday, the lassitude was close to paralysis. My legs and feet were full of lead, and I had a curious numb feeling on one side of my skull. I walked slowly, like a very old woman. Altogether strange, I thought, to be like this. In search of something, anything to interrupt the slow descent into melancholy over which I had no control, I got in the car and began driving. In previous years, the low times had not been so prolonged—work could drive them up, parties, good entertainment, good conversation. Psychiatry? Yes, on several occasions; it taught me that I had to rescue myself. Whatever happened on the outside, I had to make an inner journey.

The discovery of Wadleigh was purely fortuitous. On that August day I drove aimlessly until I was tired and hot from the sun beating in my window. The college lay at the far end of a pleasant town, and I stopped, soothed by the quiet, the coolness of old shade trees, red brick mellowed by time, white columns, and ivy.

I sat for awhile listening to the faint rustling of the leaves; then I drove in and parked the car in the welcome shade. Memory was stirring. I had been born on the campus of Willamette University in Salem, Oregon, where my father was president in 1908-1914; the child in me responded to that time, the first years of my life, much of it spent walking on lush green grass like this. Maypoles with colored ribbons, picnics, music, ladies in long white dresses and wide straw hats, my father's hand holding mine.

I rested. I was aware of a growing curiosity. What went on behind those tall windows? Would all the doors be locked?

The door to the administration building was not locked. I went in and wandered about, looking at the old portraits hanging in a large room, at serene spaces, at muted sea colors. More curious now, I walked down a long hall and found one door open where the deans' secretary was alone, typing away at a staccato rate.

There were a few hesitating amenities, but almost without warning I said, "I am looking for a job." She appeared surprised and interested. There was only one possibility, house resident. I made out a lengthy application form. The dean of students was away; they would let me know.

For the following two weeks I waited, becoming anxious again; it was too late in the summer to hope for anything else in the academic world, and my energy was dwindling more day by day. I was a tired swimmer grasping at a piece of lumber in a heavy tide. Should I have looked for a more prestigious four-year college or university? But I think now we have an intuition for what we need; I was not out for intellectual stiumulation, but for emotional healing—and to obtain a job at sixty is not an easy thing.

The young had sometimes exasperated me, but I had never been afraid of them; they had never depressed me. A zoo keeper is not afraid of lions or monkeys, from whom, I dare say, he learns a great deal.

After two weeks, there were more interviews, and the job was given to me. They were reluctant to take on a stranger, but they had not found anyone to live in Bixby dorm. A house mother, I discovered, had no professional or social status in the academic world (unless she was a member of the faculty); therefore, her role was not clearly defined. The task of living in a dormitory was not definable even by the predilections of academia for job descriptions, *curriculum vitae,* course syllabi, or committee reports. *Mirabile dictu!* The house mother, in the late sixties, was a vestigial remnant left over from college days with chaperones on each floor if "young ladies" were concerned; she was soon to become obsolete.

The dean of students, a small, kindly woman with dark eyes, gave me no specific directions, and I was given enough time off; in view of the miniscule salary, they complied with my one condition. I would be given a studio out of the dorm for writing. I was entering a foreign territory where I was advised

16

to be "an invisible woman." But paradoxically enough, I was to become visible.

To any woman living comfortably in her accustomed roles within the boundaries of old associations, it may perhaps seem preposterous that my health began to improve. I had many fears; I was afraid of loneliness and a decline into uselessness. I was afraid of stagnation and I was afraid of death.

What happened to me when I began living in Bixby dorm was sometimes shock treatment, sometimes illumination. I was recalled to my own youth. As Aldous Huxley wrote, "Human nature does not change, or, at any rate, history is too short for any changes to be perceptible."

AUTUMN

Plunging in

Opening Day at Wadleigh Junior College in New Devon, New Hampshire, burst upon me as if a time machine had plunged me directly from 1930 to 1969; whole sections of my life had disappeared—marriage, childbearing, teaching. Perhaps this was a necessary condition for someone like myself before I would return to the past, creating an interlude in which I could learn to accept my future.

A week earlier, in a hopped-up state of euphoria, I had moved into Bixby dorm where I was to live. I had moved out of an apartment inhabited by pure old ladies, sweet ladies who sprayed the hall if I smoked, and who grieved with gentle persistence, as if widowhood were a full-time occupation. Bringing my pictures and books and my favorite chair, I settled into Bixby dorm with all the trepidation and hope of a new member of the Peace Corps.

On another of my summer journeys, I had consulted a young psychoanalyst who agreed with me that a human being experiences a crisis upon entering each new decade. "At least after thirty or forty," he said.

Before I moved, I went back to see him. I said, "I have a new job."

"*What?*" he asked. I told him. He looked upset.

"Those girls will make you nervous." Like almost everyone else I knew, he thought the college student of the late sixties was a sadistic barbarian.

I was adamant. "Sometimes I think it's a good idea to go for broke," I said, "something worth having a breakdown *about*."

By Opening Day, I was theoretically "oriented." My sitting room, which now felt quite comfortable furnished with some of my own things, was across the wide front hall from my bedroom, a small room with high ceilings next to my own bath. There had been meetings with the other house residents, a group composed of young faculty members, ladies who had lost their husbands one way or another, and two veterans, Mary Barnes and Elizabeth Wyckoff, who were destined to become close friends. The dorm, which smelled of summer and years of tradition, was relatively quiet. Six girls who were "senior counselors" arrived early to prepare for the task of advising freshmen; also Barbie, the house president. These girls had their meetings alone and I did not see much of them, but they gave me a feeling of companionship. My euphoria was something like that of a traveler who is about to set off on an exciting ocean voyage, quite oblivious of the realities of possible storms, shipwrecks, and human collisions, as well as of new mysterious diseases.

These thoughts drifted in my mind as I sat in the big living room on Opening Day dressed properly, I thought, to meet the new arrivals. The living room was quiet, with green and blue colors and chintz drapes, couches covered in green vinyl, many chairs,Impressionist prints and an elegant big fireplace with a white mantel. Forty-nine girls were to inhabit this house.

Around ten, I heard a car arriving, then more cars, and I got up and went out into the large lower hall, shaped like a T. For one awful moment I felt the claustrophobia of church receptions where I was "the minister's daughter," the symphony parties where I was "the manager's wife," and the Open House at school where at least I was myself in a somewhat laundered

22

aspect. But before I ran out the door, I was surrounded by girls who were senior counselors and by the arriving freshmen, most of them with their parents. My face froze into a smile, which stayed there for many long hours. I was "the invisible woman" that day; the senior counselors, dressed in navy blue blazers bearing the Wadleigh crest, grabbed suitcases and trudged up and down stairs, and soon the old house was filled with the heavy pounding of feet.

Barbie stood by, her strawberry blonde hair shining, constant as the North Star. That day I played my role, one which was never quite like that again, never again so mechanical.

"This is our new house resident," Barbie said at frequent intervals, for the girls arrived faster than apples tumbling from barrels, and I was greeted with apprehension as the parents looked me over and the freshmen merely stared.

Banners flew fore and aft the door announcing, "Welcome, Freshmen!" in vivid shades of red, green, blue. These signals did not distress me, for my years of teaching had inured me to such corny displays: *smile* buttons, and the "togetherness" displayed over our mantel. Barbie had created a large drawing of purple grapes with green leaves; one bunch of grapes had smiling faces and the rest were blank and pure, as if awaiting later knowledge about who would scowl, who would cry, who would scream, and who would wither. This poster proclaimed to each freshman that she was now "one of the bunch."

My first encounter was with a girl and her mother, a nervously clucking female who did not wish to part with her chick. The girl was bored and turned her face away. She was scared, too.

The mother said, "Do you keep track of when the girls get in?"

"No," I said, trying to look as if this were the most natural thing in the world. "We have an honor system."

"You must have an awful lot to do."

"I am told the girls take care of everything." This was what the dean had told me, and I didn't believe it. So I was not annoyed to be answered by an expression of mingled disbelief and fear. Privately I knew their daughters were here to sink or swim.

"When I was in college," this lady began again, and we stood there in the midst of parents in their well-cut suits, their expensive knits, their smooth hair, all of them hoping against all odds that I would stand like a dragon over the front door and the sign-in sheet at two in the morning to find out who came in late, drunk, or stoned.

But raising my voice against the din I looked more seriously at this small, anxious woman. "A college does not stand in *loco parentis,*" I said, immediately hearing a "damn" in my mind, for she did not know what I was talking about. Neither did I. I was hiding behind the philosophy of the dean. But when I was scared, I froze—I knew that; this day could not be controlled by me, yet phony reassurance was not my way. We stood there in awkward silence. The girl had been whisked off upstairs by her senior counselor. I longed for the parents to go home so I could get into comfortable clothes and abandon these pleasantries. Kids, I thought, never put up with false conversation.

I called for help. "Barbie!" And she came. I had recognized in my conferences with Barbie that she was incapable of evading an issue; moreover, she loved to help, and she had that inestimable gift, a natural warmth. When I had confessed to Barbie that I feared the girls might not like me because of my age, she laughed.

"Last year we did have a young house mother, and we got tired of having to put her to bed when she came in three sheets to the wind."

Now Barbie, after one look at me, escorted the worried mother into the living room, away from the tumult in the hall, and sat down with her. I heaved a sigh of relief. I was nervously tired. As the hours wore on, I began to take some irrational pleasure in the disorder of this day when the house expanded its creaking wood and yielded up its stiff decorum while I yielded up mine. There had been nothing quite so unnerving since the day I was a student teacher facing my first class heaving in ripples up and down as if to engulf me, a madness that ceased on the second day.

There is something to be said for a situation which rolls on and on without regard for the ego or the nerves. The senior

24

counselors were nibbling cookies and saying confidentially that their feet hurt. The house was rocking with a sense of renewal.

"Oh, what a small room!" someone sighed as she came downstairs for the fifth time. Some of the girls were shoving desks and bed frames into the hall, or lugging them with crashes and bumps down to the basement storage room. Did they want to live on the floor like Japanese? I realized with a start that they did not propose to fit their bodies into anything stiff or rigid. Perhaps they intended to line their rooms with possessions until something like a bird's nest was created, good for snuggling in blankets and listening to "rock." But what of the austere tasks of scholarship?

I stood my ground in the hall, putting out my hand and smiling just as if I knew what I was doing, but my memory of this day is one of an avant-garde film with screens projecting from all sides as well as on the ceiling and floor: heads of girls advancing and fading, mini-skirts, legs, bosoms, masses of hair streaming hither and yon, slim hips in blue jeans, sweaters like rainbows, voices laughing, voices crying, voices loud and soft, cultivated voices, brash voices, thuds, suitcases spilling open, bed frames bumping, then again eyes brown, blue, hazel. Questions: "What shall I do with this *trunk*?" "Can I change my roommate?" "*Where* is my hair dryer?" Little brothers and sisters rollicked on the floor; dogs ran in; records and radios blasted on upstairs. I see myself now as if I were looking at another person standing in the midst of all this, sorting out parents, who emerged very gradually as people who were sending their daughters here because it was "safe," away from urban environments, away from suburbia, one or two of them saying, "She wasn't ready for the university, for the really tough course." Several stood out from the affluent middle class: the teacher of retarded children, the bony woman from Maine in her old grey coat and neat hair pinned up, hardy and resolute. "My daughter is going to be a doctor," she said, "and she is here to begin her pre-med. The science department here is *very good*."

She hauled her daughter over, a thin, unsmiling girl named Kate, a feminine version of Ichabod Crane, with her dark hair sticking out in back like a brush, steel-rimmed glasses, and a cross expression. "How do you do," Kate said, and escaped, her mother softening into a smile. "It takes time to know her," she said, and left to tell Kate goodbye.

I came out of myself, and the house became real again. Barbie, the maternal one happily endowed with *joie de vivre*. A very small bony freshman girl who looked like a cricket, but did not chirp; her name was Alice Brittle. She was solemn when I called her "Alice," and said, "My friends call me Peanuts." She had a shy manner and one of the few short haircuts. In all the masses of hair, combed and uncombed, Peanuts was a refreshing sight, as if she had stepped out of my flapper period.

And there was an older girl, Ellen, tall and handsome—a girl with an air of easy sophistication, a cashmere sweater and well-tailored pants. Nonchalant. Looking back, I remember Ellen for other reasons.

By afternoon, the whole space around the quad was covered with cars. I have never entirely got over the way New Englanders park on the grass, but it makes sense in autumn because the grass will soon be covered with snow. Suddenly there erupted through our wide-open back door a round-faced, buxom female with clouds of long blonde hair, a life force bursting like fireworks. I could see through the open door a rusty blue 1950 Ford, parked so close to the entrance that it had barely missed driving into the house and up the stairs, a fantasy easy to accept once the driver had made her appearance.

She stood in the center of the hall and bellowed in a Valkyrie voice,*"Where is everybody?"* The new arrivals stood galvanized in their steps. Answering screams floated down from upstairs. In two seconds, flocks of upperclassmen rushed down. "Sweetheart!" "Baby!" "Honey!" In five minutes the hall was filled with suitcases, a sewing machine, a record player, ski boots and skis, a red upholstered chair, and a dozen or so cartons.

"Who is that?" I whispered to Barbie when she disentangled herself from the welcoming mob.

"That's Virgie. Isn't she marvelous? Her real name is Maude von Diefendorf," Barbie said, and turned away again to her duties.

26

Virgie, solid and bright in a yellow shirt and old pants, with a boy's cap over her hair, saw me, looked shy, and rushed off to register, leaving us with a traffic jam. But yes, Virgie was marvelous. I began to laugh. Returning, she yelled, "This place looks like the Plaza!" (The old house had received some fresh paint during the summer and was cleaner that day than it would be for some time.) Three girls answered her. "Wait till you see the new tile in the bathrooms!" Virgie rushed to admire the showers and returned to shout, "There has never been a john like that since I went to Korvette's." Then she and twenty or so helpers took her things upstairs, disappearing into the upper reaches of the second or third floor.

I went out to inspect the car. It proclaimed on its rear end, "WADLEIGH OR BUST" in white paint. Peering inside, I saw Paisley corduroy seat covers and a blue floor carpet. For a few minutes, I stood breathing in the crisp fall air of New Hampshire. I could hear in my ears the quickness of my pulse.

When I went back in the house, I saw a father who had broken down and was sitting on the living room sofa holding his bald head between his hands while he stared at the floor. "She won't even speak to me," he said. I sat down with him for a few minutes; sometimes sitting down and listening is all one can do. But he said no more.

I got up and went to find his daughter, Leslie, sitting on a straight chair in her room, quite immobile, with a purple felt hat on her head. She wouldn't speak to me, either. This parting scene is so strange to remember now, for Les was never like that again.

"I think she is just trying to cope with all this in her own way," I said to her father, "and she will. Give her a little more time." I must have been talking about myself! He got up and left rather soon after that.

From time to time, as we continued through the day, the carillon in the bell tower rang out its mellow notes, and at last the sun shone level through the western windows. It was quiet with everyone upstairs unpacking, except for the rock that blared from every window. I could imagine the freshmen timidly filling their desks and bureau drawers and looking at their roommates with misgivings. Here were people they had to live with whether they liked it or not, and nothing short of spiritual or physical attempts at murder would persuade the dean to alter the arrangements.

I thought about my day. I could not explain to the parents why I was not terrified of living with forty-nine girls in a world of defiance, pot, race riots, bombs. One mother had departed fearfully because she discovered that we did not lock the doors at night. I could not help feeling that we were experiencing the last of an era, a time of overlapping the old with the new, and that anything was better than sitting on the sidelines and moaning. For a little while, I might expect the girls to give me a wide berth. I represented the dangerous unknown chemical in our society—"an old person."

By evening, all the parents who had stayed to take their daughters out for a *bon voyage* dinner had disappeared, sometimes waving until they were out of sight, and daughters who were not crying came in with expressions of relief. By eight o'clock they were all in the living room hearing Barbie tell them about the rules, and for the first and last time they sat primly on couches and chairs. They all sang the alma mater lustily and began to realize they were part of something that had been here since it began in an old Academy down the street in 1837. By 9:30, they were all huddled down in their rec room in the basement watching "The Endless Summer" on TV.

Out of a memory of my boarding school days I did a rather strange thing that night; I went upstairs and told each one good night as our corridor teacher did—and then I went to bed and slept in spite of the noise. The next morning I realized that my insomnia had been temporarily cured. The night watchman clumped through the halls and up the stairs several times, and I found this comforting. When I woke up, I looked around my bedroom which contained my chest of drawers, my bed, and a small table and easy chair. The toaster and coffee pot sat on the table; I had decided I would not go to breakfast in the commons.

Somewhere outside, I heard a gravelly voice—Virgie—saying, "I can't wait to tell them all the *bad* stuff," and I could almost see her rubbing her hands. What was the "bad stuff"?

The sun was out, and I could see through my window the shapes of trees. There was a slight tap on my door, as much as to say, "It is nine o'clock," and it really was. I climbed out of bed, put on my robe, and opened the door, feeling rather like a lazy slattern as I saw our maid, Mrs. Perley, a seventy-year-old blue angel in her pale blue nylon uniform. She was round, soft, and buxom.

"Do you want me to do your room?" she said, and picked up her old straw basket of cleaning aids from the settle outside my door.

"Just this once. But after this, I will do it except once a week when you are vacuuming—only it's a good thing for you to tap on my door in case I have overslept." It seemed to me this was a good time to have a chat with Mrs. Perley. I sat down in the easy chair and watched her make my bed and dust with a clean old bit of rag.

"Are you a native New Englander, Mrs. Perley?"

"Oh, yes. We had a farm, you know, but my husband died of cancer a long time ago—I still live in the big farmhouse and my sons help me out when I need them."

There was something about Mrs. Perley that was soothing, as if I had known her before.

"I was a postmistress," she volunteered. She was not tight-lipped, but she spoke succinctly in a kindly voice. I watched her quick, economical movements as she "did" my room with rapid movements, flicking away disorder.

Her hair was blonde—really not possible? Her wise eyes were as blue as her dress.

"What can I do to help you?" I said. She leaned on the mop handle.

"Well, get those skis out of the hall, for one thing. If you don't, we will be falling over them all winter. They are supposed to keep the skis in the basement. I've carried some of them down. And I collect all the toothbrushes and towels and soap--shampoo—everything like that, if they leave them in the bathrooms."

"What do you do with them?"

She sparkled. "I lock them up in my closet in the basement, and they can't get them back unless they come to me personally." A mischievous look passed between us. "And I am here personally only in the *morning*."

A wise woman. I looked at Mrs. Perley with awe. Her pride went deeper than the job she was doing, one could feel that; yet she was doing her job with a minimum of fuss and a maximum of humor. I felt we would be allies .

"Have you got any children?" she inquired unexpectedly.

"Yes, two, and six grandchildren." I expected the conventional question, "What are you doing *here?*" but Mrs. Perley did not inquire further. Her manners were impeccable. I did not need to give a hedging answer or even a real one, which might have been that my children and I were all in a period when I felt they might work out their own problems without me breathing down their necks . . . or was that the whole answer? I was a maverick grandmother.

"And you?" I said.

"Oh, I have twelve grandchildren, and so many great-grandchildren that I can hardly keep up!" she said, meanwhile gathering up her things and going to the door, where she turned to give me a reassuring look.

"Don't worry about the girls—they are really *good* girls," she concluded in a tone as mild as fresh milk, and went out, softly closing the door.

This encounter with Mrs. Perley made me feel I had a partner I could count on. Every morning she would be there to give us a clean, fresh start. With Mrs. P. in the morning and Barbie in the evening, I began to hope I might make it. I made my toast and coffee and sat down to the obbligato of feet running up and down stairs, doors beginning to slam, and voices saying they had to register, buy books, and they would *not* eat eggs or oatmeal no matter what.

Then I went in the bathroom and there I was in the mirror, looking like an old child, with grey eyes and brown hair that somehow had not turned grey as it was supposed to. Once dressed in pants and a sweater (for I did not propose to be a "lady" except in the afternoons) I went out and pussy-footed my way across the hall.

A black girl came jumping down the first floor corridor, leaping high in the air, her arms held up, yelling, "I am Maria—who are you?" Maria was an apparition suddenly appearing from nowhere. Where was she yesterday?

"I am the only black girl on this campus," Maria said with a certain air of distinction as she shook my hand cordially, "and I got here late last night."

The *only* black girl? How benighted was this place, anyway? Maria stood there, beaming a wide grin. "I'm not really black—I'm Jamaican." She was a soft *cafe au lait* in color and very beautifully boned. "But a real black girl is coming." Maria seemed intent on filling me in on some things I already knew from studying the list of my charges. "She's from Biafra, and she's coming because the University of Nigeria was bombed out."

I could not tell from Maria's expression whether she was gratified to welcome someone from Biafra, or rather annoyed at the prospect of losing her unique status. She was breathtaking, dynamic, someone to reckon with, but as I was realizing all this, she took off as fast as she had come. With a sigh of relief, I walked over to my studio in the basement room of the dorm across the way and sat down at the desk.

Here was a real refuge, a room with windows close to the ceiling, a lock on the door, my typewriter, and that one object so dear to my heart, a very *big* table for my work. There was also a bathroom, an empty closet, and a college cot. This was my bomb shelter where I could spend my mornings or burrow when things got beyond my powers of composure. This was my secret, not to be discovered by the girls for months to come, and I resolved never to admit anyone into it.

The sun was sifting through the high windows, and here, away from everything, I heard only the booming of the old furnace boiler. I wanted to think about this plunging world I found myself in, and I began to take notes. What am I doing here, I thought. Why do I like it?

The dean's voice came back to me, "You must not mother

the girls. They hate being fussed over. They are also sensitive to indifference. Wait until they come to you and then treat them like adults." (But they *weren't* adults. They did not seem like adults. Only Barbie.)

"'Teach me to care and not to care,'" I had said, thinking of T. S. Eliot.

"Precisely."

Well, hmmm. At the moment I was more interested in myself than the girls, most of whom were ignoring me. Various disconnected thoughts drifted through my mind. . . . I did not feel like a vacuum now. . . . I was homesick for my children . . . the psychiatrist at Dartmouth had said I reminded him of his mother, so we parted company. . . . I could not bear to correct another English paper with all those little squiggles, notes, succeeding conferences and *grades*. A nagging thought—could it be that when I walked in here I was saying, "I want to come home?" What a trick of the unconscious! Or even more, "I want to be renewed."

This sounded so absolutely wild that I got up, put on my coat, went out and locked the door. It was time for lunch, and as I walked across the quad I decided I really did not care why I was here because I felt better. I didn't have to get meals, clean the house, catch buses, or entertain . . . and there was a library. And I was not alone. Girls were streaming across the campus, and one of them held open the door of the commons for me.

The Wadleigh World

The commons was located in the lower floor of the library, and the stairs were crowded wall to wall with hungry girls. In front of me was Miss Barnes, a house resident at Canby dorm, who also had a full-time teaching load. She was that *rara avis*, an exotic New Englander, with coppery hair and great dash and style; I had met her at our preliminary meetings.

She turned, smiled, and said, "Follow me." Miss Barnes pushed politely, if such a thing is possible, through the dense crowd with all the finesse of a fast quarterback who has the ball, saying, however, "Excuse us, please," on every step. The bodies parted as if by magic to let us through, although the faces looked as faces always look when the brass commands.

There were some six hundred girls who ate in the commons, and the noise was like the twittering of six hundred blackbirds in a flock. Faculty members and house residents were seated at several round tables close to a window overlooking the back campus, which sloped away down a green hill toward a backdrop of leaves now turning into vivid color. This was the only place on campus where I would meet with adults very often.

The conversation rose to a shrill crescendo inside the commons, and I observed the girls from Bixby dorm clannishly sitting together. I could identify Barbie, Ellen, Peanuts, Kate, Leslie, Maria, but most of the names escaped me.

Now I always keep up with Mary Barnes and Elizabeth Wyckoff, who became my permanent guides. We still have dinner together several times a year; they belonged to an intrepid company of house mothers who lived on year in and year out in the dorms and sometimes took on other dorms as guidance counselors, for house mothers were an endangered species. Mary was open and talkative, still in her forties; I think of her with her pale copper hair, amber eyes, creamy skin, dressed in the colors she always wears, gold, green, brown, coral. Mary ran a dorm of over two hundred girls with the genius of an exceptionally good master sergeant, delegating authority and seeing that her orders were carried out to the letter.

Now she said brightly, "How are you doing?" as we began on our salad and our ham and cheese sandwiches. She made introductions.

"I don't really know," I said. Not a whit deterred, Mary launched into a story of her summer in Africa where she had supervised a teaching program for "Crossroads." I was impressed. She had taken some Wadleigh girls along.

Elizabeth Wyckoff was tall, slender, and greying, a widow who was teaching in the science department lab and living in a dorm, my contemporary. She had spent the summer in Japan, where she had been born to missionary parents. "And I saw the village where I was born," she exclaimed with delight, "and there were some very old people there who remembered me, and we were even invited in for tea!"

I began to look around at the people who were new to me, although the din was distracting. There was a professor of political science and a young couple with a baby in a high chair who were both living in Oliver dorm while he worked on a Ph.D. from Dartmouth, a divorced lady with a little girl about two years of age, a witty English professor, and a very polite gentleman from India.

34

It was at the table in the commons that I soon became aware of the status of a house resident who was not a member of the faculty; my impressions may have been partly the result of my temperament. I can reveal myself only by small degrees and have a face inherited from my Anglo-Saxon ancestors, a rather mild, undistinguished face that easily melts into the herd and does not at once proclaim that even if I invite confidences, I have a fierce temper and an unsettling intensity. I have formed these conclusions after a lifetime of having strangers ask me if I were someone's secretary, or whether I could give directions to a given location, or hear a tale of woe. My son said to me when he was three years old, "When you nod your head, I know you are not listening." Despite this ear opener, I still nod my head.

I nodded my head all through lunch. To my astonishment, I "heard" more hostility toward the students, then and at other meals, than I would have believed possible, but never from Mary or Elizabeth, who related the anecdotes of their dorm life with delightful humor. I remembered that the "shop talk" when I had lunch with my colleagues during my professional days was inevitably discouraging; sometimes I wonder if doctors, nurses, dentists, have quite the same need to groan over the administration, the relatives, and the patients as do members of the teaching profession.

But now Miss Barnes was lightening the gloom of those who feared Wadleigh had taken on too many students with mediocre College Board scores. "Just imagine," she said, "I once had a girl who brought a donkey into the dorm and tried to take it upstairs! Such pulling and hauling you never saw. So I painted an abstract portrait of a donkey and gave it to her for graduation."

Elizabeth chimed in. "We have a boy friend I found in a girl's bed. He wants to live with us, and there they were, snoozing like two lambs."

"Well, we have four hippies in our basement and I *have* to get them out," Mary said. "They are awfully hairy, but nice and gentle. I guess they got in before we arrived."

The faculty who had their own domestic arrangements off campus took a dim view of these stories. One complained that the girls no longer dressed for dinner. Another said too many were "dumb" and never should have been admitted; most of them would marry young. "I get so *tired*," a young man said, "of trying to get a response. When I came back this year, I got sick at my stomach."

Mary remarked with sardonic humor, "We have to fill the beds—remember?"

A large dog wandered in and the girls at the nearest table began feeding him from their plates. "O, he's licking my toes!" There were shrieks and wiggles. A storm of protest arose, and the hostess of the commons dragged him out by the collar. "Pets!" It sounded as if we might expect an influx of dogs, cats, hamsters throughout the year even if the rules expressly forbade the invasion of animal life into our living quarters.

Someone remarked, "I know a house mother who had goldfish in her sitting room, and the girls took them out of the bowl and presented them to her *cooked*—on a plate, of course. It's no wonder she left."

My heart skipped a beat and stopped, even though I am addicted to plants, not fish. The conversation was becoming banal, not to say terrifying, as if some of these people were in the wrong business and considered it their duty to warn me of the horrors to come. If it had not been for the memory of teachers who do not like children (sadists who sprinkle themselves among true spirits in every profession) my apprehension would have dived down to the level of panic.

I saw that Mary and Elizabeth shared my thoughts; I saw it in their eyes, which clearly said, "Get tough." They were both members of a special breed, people who recognize other people without being told why they should do so. I had reason to know later on that Mary could cope with a fire in the dorm set off by a girl who let a candle burn while she slept, and with another girl who was driving when one of her friends was killed in a car accident and became so morbid that she wore her dead friend's clothes for weeks. All this inspired Mary to kind sympathy and positive action.

Mary's eyes, her smile, reflected a natural trust. Elizabeth, who was extremely modest, glanced my way with a quizzical, wise look, and I got the message.

36

From this day on, I went to the commons only once a day, for dinner. I went to the market and bought things for my breakfast and lunch, stowing them in a tiny refrigerator in a corner of my sitting room. In the old days I had taken my lunch to school to gain thirty minutes of quiet. I didn't like the hurly-burly or the press of bodies then, either. I required a chance to eat quietly.

What was the "Wadleigh World"? During the year I came to know very little of it. I did not go often to the administration building except to get my mail in the college post office or to see one of the deans. I had a passing acquaintance with the nurses in the infirmary. The faculty remained almost entirely unknown to me, except at the arts center where I took a drawing class and very much enjoyed it. For awhile I was assigned as an advisor to the Student Alumnae Fund organization and made halfhearted attempts to supervise the snack bar in the arts center, "for fear you wouldn't have enough to do," the dean of students said. Later the dean of the college helped me find some work in the alumnae office. But on the whole, my world was limited to Bixby dorm, the place where I was vitally interested. It was within these confines that I came to believe that the emotional growth of students has as much to do with "why they are in college" as the development of their minds; in the dorm I saw them as I had never seen them in the classroom: quite open to the struggle of learning how to live with others, how to get along, how to get ready for a tough old world. It was a fortunate coincidence that I was trying to learn something also: how to approach my later years in a spirit of acceptance and activity.

Did Wadleigh have quality? One can only compare it with others of its kind, junior colleges, in-between places as junior high schools are, which serve their purpose. I think within this context, Wadleigh did have "class." It was aesthetically satisfying and the staff was dedicated to getting out of the students the maximum of which they were capable. The curriculum embraced both courses designated as terminal—such as preparation for executive secretaries and medical technologists (to be followed by work experience)—and courses that would lead to transfer to a university for degrees in liberal arts or science. I met one girl who had spent a whole summer studying James Joyce at Dartmouth, and she told me she had found her Wadleigh preparation stimulating.

Moreover, the environment of Wadleigh had a certain fastidiousness: a consciousness of tradition, kind manners, the serenely proportioned architecture of the classical revival. Of course students wore jeans and patches and put their bare feet up on chairbacks. Nevertheless, I have learned from the memories of alumnae that at Wadleigh they had acquired a certain respect for unpretentious elegance as well as for learning. Snobbishness was not part of the scene, neither socially nor intellectually. There were girls from India, Hawaii, Thailand, Africa, California, Florida, with a heavy concentration from the New England states. I heard about "the Wadleigh girl," a mythical being much sought after by the admissions office, and at first I thought she must be imaginary; however, twelve years later, I can identify Wadleigh girls when I see them walking down the streets of New Devon, although they are dissimilar in dress and physique. They have a certain distinction impossible to define, and not identifiable by ordinary standards.

Despite the complaints I heard all year about how perfectly terrible it was to be marooned up here in the country where there was "nothing to do," I saw the college making valiant attempts to provide concerts, plays, lectures, art shows, movies, "mixers." In the best tradition, the town and gown were united, for most of these events brought to the town as well as to the college a great deal of what is good in the outside world. It is to Wadleigh's credit, I think, that I never saw any graffiti on the walls, and that flowers were planted in spring.

I walked through the streets of New Devon many times in all kinds of weather. The business establishments were housed in white frame buildings, and the old houses were each spaced at a respectful distance from its neighbor, that each might enjoy all aspects of the sunlight and a free flow of clean air. Restrictions on zoning preserved this lovely spareness, along with the New England Town Meeting and the native pride in working at a neat landscape uncluttered by people who do not care. I got to know the druggist, the grocery clerks, the doctors, the florist, the little dress shops, and they got to know me. It was heartening to have a Wadleigh alumna who owned a sports shop *insist* that I must have a suede jacket lined with sheepskin. "It's the very warmest thing and I don't care *how* you pay for it!" I still love this old jacket. I went to Hanover once a week for a change; there, where Dartmouth was the center of the town, I found another place I loved. And I could go to Boston or New York, only to return feeling thankful that up to this time, we did not have a problem with hard drugs or general decay.

I settled in to the year of many surprises, a year when I learned that fashions change, dangers change, society changes, but the primal experiences of life which involve our deepest emotions—our fears, our angers, our loves, our hates, our joys, do not change. "How I wish," Max Beerbohm once said, "I could keep up with these fashions which pass by me into oblivion."

Barbie Counsels Me

Gradually the days took on a form, as days have a way of doing where most of the people involved operate on fixed schedules. I could do as I liked, and I wrote in my notes or journals or worked on an occasional poem in the mornings, took a nap in the afternoons to recover from the late nights, did errands, and around five o'clock dressed for dinner and sat in the living room or in my sitting room with the door open, ready for some conversation. But it was in the evenings that most of the dorm activity took place: meetings after dinner, study hours from 7:00 to 10:00, a wild explosion called "noisy hour" from 10:00 to 10:30, and then more study hours. Very often the girls who should have been studying sat with me and looked at TV, talking all the while, the way the young do today, as if the TV provided them with a cover.

In the evening some girls signed out and some came home late. It seemed to me that the most critical discussions, the most painful crises, cropped up around midnight or later. During the afternoon or early evening I seemed to be there to lend to some impatient soul a screwdriver, a hammer, an extension cord, a band-aid, or a bit of thread—everything from a vase for flowers or a candlestick, down to a medical thermometer or a heating pad. Occasionally there was a frantic plea to be permitted to go into my sitting room and lock the door, "Because *people* are driving me crazy."

And as all this went on, day by day, the girls emerged, whether I got their names straight or not. That is, most of them. There were a few girls I never really got to know at all; for example, one who made a practice of staying out nights until the very last minute, and one who never appeared on the lower floor except to go through and up to her room. I heard that she studied constantly, sitting on her bed in a Buddha posture.

In all this, I relied on Barbie, who came in for evening conferences, more to "clue me in" than because she needed guidance. Barbie, I concluded, was the real house mother, the one who took all the "flak," and I was the grandmother; not so strange when I reflected that my oldest grandchild, Vivian, was now in her teens.

I had to cross the wide hall to go from my bedroom to my sitting room, an awkward situation, but one which had the fringe benefit of permitting me to keep my bedroom a very private place. From the very first evening after the freshmen arrived, the hall was populated with boys, as if they knew when to visit as well as tomcats do. It was a trial to the new girls to descend the stairs and be looked over by appraising eyes, but the second night five of them were toted off and returned inebriated. One girl fell down in the middle of the hall, waved her arms and sang.

Barbie said after I made the mistake of going out in my robe to see what was going on, that I must stay in my room amid the scuffles, the stumbles, and the long, lingering farewells. Barbie was the interpreter of the law, and the law, at this time, said that a girl might not drink on campus, but we could scarcely follow her off campus.

A few days later, Barbie appeared at my sitting room in the evening, and I put down my book. Her presence was radiant. She was nearly always in blue jeans, a navy sweat shirt and sneakers fashionably filthy, or run-over loafers; she was a girl who was rather plump and bosomy with very clean long fair hair and bright blue eyes—almost Juno-esque.

"This room is nice," Barbie said. I had brought with me my private fetishes. An old oriental coral rug lay on the blue carpeting. I had a Chinese embroidery, framed, on the wall, and I was sitting in my favorite blue armchair with a high back, next to a bookcase full of the books I felt I had to take with me wherever I went. Barbie walked around the room, looking intently at the new objects, and holding in her hands the smaller things, such as a sculptured cat, a crystal paperweight. Finally she took up something that looked like a hen's egg in size, a greyish ceramic inlaid with tiny stones from a California beach—a present on Easter.

"How on earth was this made?" she said, holding it and turning it to get the feeling of it in her hand.

"I don't know—it's a mystery to me." I perceived that Barbie had a tactile sense. "Are you interested in art?"

She blushed disarmingly. "I'm nuts about ceramics. But I'm studying to be a med tech. Laboratory stuff in medicine."

Ignoring the love seat and a rocking chair, she sat down in the middle of the room and crossed her legs under her.

"I'm still full of hang-ups," I said. "How are things going upstairs?"

"Well, for one thing, the water in the second floor showers was overflowing and leaking downstairs, and I went over to the custodians and told them about it. They said the drains were stopped up because we have so much *hair*. Pooh. We haven't been here long enough for that! They are coming over in the morning to fix whatever it is."

I could hear the boys rumbling in the hall and got up and shut the door.

"How am I doing?" I said, relieved to hear that a shower could get fixed behind my back.

Barbie rolled over on her back and crossed her arms under her head. She looked ruminative.

"O.K. They think you are cool."

"Thank you," I said with feeling.

"The freshmen are a pretty good lot. Tomorrow night they

will get their Big Sisters and their beanies. We've had them write down whoever they would like for a Big Sister, three choices, and the seniors do the same for Little Sisters. It's fantastic how often they can be matched up, when they hardly know each other yet. One or two are screaming to me that they don't like their roommates, but the dean won't let them change for a long time."

It still seemed a bit strange to me that as this was a junior college, we had only freshmen and seniors, but I had observed that being called a senior seemed to relieve a sophomore of sophomoric behavior.

There was a knock on the door. "Come in," I said. The door opened and a rather thin, stringy girl stood there.

"When is Victoria coming?" she asked without preamble. "I'm lonesome in my room all by myself."

Barbie sat up. "In about a week."

The door closed. "That's Rae. She's a freshman and she was picked to be Victoria's roommate because her application showed a lot of 'social concern' and all that stuff. Victoria is a black girl from Biafra—she was going to the University of Nigeria, but it was bombed out and she lost all her records, so she couldn't get into a university here. She wrote me a letter. Wow, can she write a letter! My art teacher who is a Quaker talked the college into taking her."

Suddenly I remembered Rae, who had been introduced to me on the first day; she had held up two fingers in the peace sign and said, "*Pax vobiscum,*" startling me considerably.

"Rae's a funny kid," Barbie went on, rolling back on the floor as if relaxation was the secret of her success, "not run-of-the-mill at all. We don't know her very well yet."

I could think of ten more questions to ask, but Barbie got up. The interview was over. "I have to get to the books; see you later." She beamed a smile at me. "Don't worry about the sign-outs. I check the book every night before I go to bed. After they get in late three times, we have them up before the house council." And she went out.

For five minutes I thought once again of Mrs. Ramsey. "She could be herself, by herself. . . . To be silent; to be alone . . ." and just as I got up to take *To the Lighthouse* from my bookcase, I heard a wild explosion of screams, shouts, thundering feet, and music breaking out from assorted record players—over me, under me, and all around me, as if the house had turned into a brawling nightclub on New Year's Eve.

But it was only noisy hour, ten o'clock, and I opened my door to see a tall, dark girl flying through the hall dressed in a flowered flannel nightgown, with her hair in big pink rollers, a sight which the boys absorbed calmly. One of them yelled, "Have you got any cigarettes?"

"Sure," she answered, looking flushed and pretty, "I'll throw down a pack over the banister when I go back upstairs."

"Get dressed and come on out," he said.

"Maybe. See you later."

I glanced at her as she ran back upstairs, carrying a bottle of Coke. It was Ellen, the same dignified, suave Ellen I had seen once before, carrying her suitcase.

The boys looked at me with a definite, unanimous distaste, as if I were an old harridan bent on disrupting their sex life. They were an assorted lot, some with beards or moustaches and long hair, others rather neat and clean, one with a Dartmouth sweater. There were about ten of them sitting on the two settles outside my bedroom door or sprawled on the floor, very much at home. By this time the hall was also filled with girls in various states of disarray, in nightgowns, robes, or pants and sweatshirts. They didn't look romantic.

The boys were looking as if the female at home was a nourishing sight, and all they asked of life was to undress the girls and enjoy the sight of the female form. The hall breathed an ambience of sex.

Rae, who only minutes before had been in the doorway of the sitting room, flitted through in a transparent, diaphanous Indian sari, producing a dramatic sensation. She did not look to the right or left, but simply swooped on the wings of her sleeves into the living room, causing at least one boy to whistle a wolf call.

My phone was ringing in my bedroom, and I went to answer it. Mary Barnes. "I have a cottage at the lake and we'll

44

get together there when the birches turn golden." I thanked her and hung up. I was determined to go to bed and ignore the racket, which subsided by eleven as if to encourage me. Before I went to sleep, I thought about Rae, and then listened to the wind in the trees.

Rae Introduces Willie

Somehow, since the human being adapts to what must be, or else gives up, I became accustomed to a ballet swirling around me at certain times of day, and to knocks on my door at unlikely moments. The noise was something else. There were times in those early days, before I knew the girls well enough, that I was hesitant even to ask politely if they would *not* play rock over my head at nap time. I am convinced that a real display of fake authority would have alienated them from me permanently.

The next afternoon right after I had finished my solitary lunch, there was a knock. It was Rae. She looked sad but inquiring, an Oliver Twist look, someone on a quest for something she could not name. She was sleek in striped brown hip-hugger pants, a brisk cotton shirt and suede-fringed moccasins.

"Would you take me to the market today to buy some things for a party tonight? Willie just got engaged to Robert last night." Heavens. So soon in the year? "After the freshmen get their beanies, we want to give Willie a party during noisy hour."

This was the first request for my services. The car! Of course. "How about four o'clock?" I said.

46

She grinned. "Great," and she was off before I could say another word.

We got to the market on schedule. Rae was fussy about the cake. She finally got two from Pepperidge Farms and large cans of pink Kool-Aid, birthday candles, crepe paper, and balloons. As if this were not enough to satisfy her idea of fun, she bought herself some gum drops and licorice strings.

"Have some penny candy?" She looked quite cheerful now. My stomach turned over. When I was six I loved jujubes and paraffin bottles filled with juice, but now the prospect conjured up red sugar around the mouth and lint in the pockets.

"No, thank you," I said. I would have preferred a very dry vodka martini.

On the way back, Rae burbled. "I'm so *happy* this year. I'm so *involved*." This was at variance with the way I saw her.

"What are you involved with?" But she was looking me over.

"Say, you look great in your bell-bottom pants. Real cool."

"They aren't a new idea," I said. "Marlene Dietrich wore them in the 1940s."

She hadn't answered my question. "Involved with what?" I said again.

"Oh, religious discussions. I'm very interested in God." There was a pause while I felt myself biting on the Rock of Ages cleft for me, and looked hard at a woman raking up leaves. "And boycotts on the Vietnam war, and saving the environment."

"That sounds like a large order."

"Well, I'm very busy all the time. Say, would you take my winter coat to the cleaners some day? It's so dirty, and I forgot to get it cleaned before I came. And the weather will get cold all of a sudden. I'm just crazy about my winter coat."

"Yes, just this once." This gal was looking for her mother.

When we got back and carried in the groceries, it developed that they must all be stowed in a far corner of my sitting room "so the girls won't eat the stuff before tonight." Rae ran upstairs and came back with a fake fur coat that appeared to have been through several back-packing trips, or perhaps dragged across a floor covered with coal dust. It was once brown and white, and now she clasped it in her arms affectionately, as if it were the family dog.

I took the coat. "Are you sure you don't mind?" she asked somewhat belatedly.

"Not at all. But remember, I will get a slip for it and then you will have to find a way to get it and pay for it, O.K.? I have a little rule, not do things for one I couldn't do for all—unless you are in *real trouble*."

"All right." I went in and closed my door and looked at the coat. A security blanket! (On the other hand, when I was in college, I can't remember having any social concerns at all beyond how to get a date.) I had made a trip to the dean's office to read the applications of the girls in my dorm and had been really impressed by their social awareness. Over and over again I read in answer to the question, "What was your most exciting experience last year?" such answers as "camp counselor," "helping retarded children," "exercising handicapped children," "a protest march," "working in a ghetto—reading? "Camus," "Eldridge Cleaver," "Malcolm X."

I stood there with Rae's coat, trying to sort this out. It would be interesting to know more about her. There seemed to be a gap as wide as a canyon between the little girl and the prospective social worker. From force of habit, I felt in the pockets of the coat that was going to the cleaners. Plenty of lint, Kleenex, chewing gum, and a note signed, "Keep the faith." This last rocked me out of my temporary complacency. Peace . . . nonviolence . . . slowly, a scene in the classroom . . . Gandhi, "Treat everyone as if he is already what he would like to become."

It was the girls who were treating me as if I were what I would like to become, an older woman in command of her own life, someone to trust, ready to give, untroubled by her fears of age. This was a sobering thought. I had no doubt that they would, in time, discover my weaknesses; the young would not put up with a facade.

I can understand human beings only one by one, and time

only day by day; perhaps, to be truthful, I understand human beings only moment by moment, and time as a series of moments called *now*. I remembered, as I dressed for dinner that night, that I had no memories of life as a halcyon affair with something called happiness. I learned with my mother's milk that life was tragic, for her fifth child and first daughter was drowned when I was ten days old—an event which was supposed to have nothing to do with me, yet it eventually burdened me with a persistent compulsion to please my parents. By the time I was six, I heard of the tragedy, and by the time I was ten, my brothers were in the army of World War I. When I was sixteen, my father, a clergyman, experienced the bitterness of failure as the result of the tyranny of power in a church official. By the time I was thirty, I was divorced and poor, with two children to raise. For the next twenty-seven years I was a teacher of rebellious adolescents—for they were always rebellious, openly or secretly.

I do not look upon my youth with the nostalgia I seem to find in the remarks of my friends. It was a hard time, a difficult time, and it seemed to be so for the students I had and for my own children. It was a hard time, even though not as frightening as the world of today. We lived inside ourselves, full of romantic dreams of the future; we lived a secret life.

We lived in a small world, unaware of the rest of life on this planet, and politics was not our business. We lived in a selfish world where any subterfuge was all right if we preserved a polite exterior. For my own part, I learned to smoke, drink, wear short skirts and bobbed hair. I hid a forbidden book, *Dusty Answer,* under my mattress, although I did not understand it. It was the fashion then with parents to praise their children in public and scold them in private. Children were objects of personal pride—and children played this game. Even in 1930 some of us were living in a backwash of Victorianism which assumed sexual ignorance would be followed by a glorious enlightenment on a romantic wedding night—a night one came to as a virgin.

Those of my peers whose minds are most rigid today, whether they are bitter or complacent, are the ones who bought the dream entire. It is harder to wake up at fifty or sixty than at twenty or thirty. And part of the dream was that America was always right, generous, honorable, safe, roomy, and that this would never change. The poor were with us then, and the blacks were with us then, but only a few people raised in the middle class were more than dimly aware of them. As for bad children, they were punished. And good children were rewarded.

Now, at this very moment, as I put on my lipstick and brushed my hair, I felt that age could be a time to work on what I might become.

When I went out into the hall, Rae appeared as if she had been waiting for me. Doors were slamming upstairs and girls were running out to dinner.

"It's noise pollution," she wailed. "Why can't they shut a door without slamming it?" A good question. I had ever heard so many slamming doors in my life.

"The girls want you to come to the party for Willie's engagement," she said. "Will you?"

I felt I had made some social progress, something that never fails to cheer the disenchanted heart, however much we pretend to disdain it. "I'd love to come," I said, and meant it. "Where and when?"

"In my room at ten o'clock."

We walked over to dinner together, mostly in silence. The quad was lit with evening lamps, and the sky had the fiery afterglow of an autumn sunset.

At dinner that evening I learned that Mrs. Wyckoff (who told me to call her Elizabeth) as well as Mary Barnes had her own escape hatch. Elizabeth had an apartment across the street from the campus.

Dinner was veal parmigiana and broccoli, with jello salad and ice cream for dessert. I thought the veal did not resemble anything I had tasted before.

"This always seems like rubber," Elizabeth said, with a moue of distaste. "Sometime we will have dinner at *my* place when this is on the menu."

50

"I rent my cottage to skiers when the snow flies," Mary added, "but I have guests once in a while until then."

These overtures were pleasant.

"What shall I do tonight when the girls get their beanies?" I asked, for I understood that this was a ceremony of sorts.

"Nothing, really, or you might hang around in the shadows nearby if you would like to see what happens."

It promised to be a busy evening. For the remainder of the dinner hour it was shop talk, and I discovered that I was lucky to have Barbie for a house president.

"That girl will get the award for Wadleigh Girl of the Year—mark my word," Mary said.

The old customs persisted in 1969. Right after dinner the freshmen were penned up in their rooms, to which they meekly retreated when the seniors yelled, "Go to your rooms and stay there!" Huddling like scared squirrels, they were quiet until two seniors went up the stairs and brought them down two by two and herded them into my little sitting room. There I was required to sit. Shades of hazing days! I was told I must look stern and give a lecture to these twenty-six trembling children on how "disappointed" the seniors were in them. I saw in the eyes of the freshmen that they would have their revenge at the first opportunity.

In the living room the seniors all lined up in two long lines at right angles to the big fireplace, dressed in their traditional navy blue. The house was plunged in darkness except for an orange candle burning on the mantel. Behind their backs the seniors held navy freshmen "beanies."

I left the freshmen in my sitting room and went out to stand in the hall near the front door which had been locked, and periodically I had to open it in answer to pounding from the boys, who wanted to know "What the hell was going on?"

The seniors came, one at a time, to take a freshman out to walk between the two rows of seniors. Each freshman received a beanie, and went to kneel behind a senior; each was solemnly adjured never to be without her beanie upon her head, even in the shower.

A rift in tradition appeared. One girl responded to all this clap-trap by saying she did not come here to join the Girl Scouts and she intended to wear her beanie at all times with a shower cap over it, even in classes. I felt sympathetic with her.

The ceremonies over, there was a great deal of screaming, weeping, and laughing, as the Big Sisters embraced their Little Sisters and they all repaired to the Butt, a smoking room in the basement. Of all things, dusky Maria was the Big Sister to Leslie, the palest of the lot, the one who wouldn't speak to her father on Opening Day. Both of them seemed overjoyed at this arrangement and danced around, quite "turned on."

I arrived at the party in Rae's room at ten as the nightly riot began, although in truth this evening it had been going on previously in the Butt for at least an hour. I felt that my presence put something of a damper on the festivities. For one thing, I was still dressed in shoes with heels, panty hose, earrings, beads, and a dress, while the party-goers were sprawled around in their nightgowns in every corner of the floor. I was greeted by two girls who yelled simultaneously that I should help them write a short story for a "creative writing" course, thus interjecting academia into a social occasion. But as this was the first indication that they had heard teaching had been my profession, I did not object.

Ellen was standing up, wearing a bright red sweat shirt over her nightgown. "We have to write a story about a child, and I do not want to write a story about a child; I don't want to remember about being a child."

In the noisy confusion, I tried to answer and get off the subject for the present. "Write about what annoyed you." She became silent.

The room was strung with crepe paper which was holding up balloons blown up to perhaps one-third of their possible capacity; how did this happen? The lung power in the dorm was enough to fill a dirigible. The balloons, a bit wrinkled, were bright with kindergarten colors.

Barbie, who was fully dressed in her jeans and navy blazer, got up like a lady who has just dropped in, and said she had "another engagement." Everyone hooted. (It saddened me to think that in the future some of these girls would become ladies and learn to make polite noises.)

Willie, the guest of honor, was lying on a bed and showed me the roses her mother had sent for her engagement celebration. She was a tall, thin, very pale blonde with glasses; I had noticed her only superficially and thought her rather colorless. Her hair was always neatly brushed back and tied with a ribbon. She wore no make-up and had the innocent look of a happy mouse. I thought of Willie as shy, and noticed that she spoke beautiful English and was very polite.

Now, as Willie held out the pink roses, I smelled them. "MMMMMMM."

Under the cover of conversation, Willie said in a soft little voice, "I would like you to meet my mother. You may not remember, but you met my father when he drove me down from Maine. He's very handsome and has white hair, kind of elegant."

"What does your mother do?" I asked.

"She's a doctor. She is divorced from my father, and we had to move out of our wonderful old house, and now we live in a kind of tumbledown one by the ocean. But she seems to be contented."

"How does your father live?"

"Oh, he went off with a much younger woman, and then he married her, and now he doesn't like her any more. And he wants us back, but my mother doesn't want to go back with him."

I glanced at the other girls, all of whom were deep in gossip and giggling. I was surprised. I would never have picked Willie for a situation like this.

"What do you do when you go home to see them?"

"Oh, my father lives only a short distance from us, and I visit back and forth."

The girls were looking at us now, and the private conversation ceased as Rae bore the cakes in from my sitting room and began counting heads as cries came up—"I want chocolate!" "I want lemon!" Rae, who had created a tea table from a packing box, glowed with satisfaction; her face relaxed into smiles, and for a moment I saw the woman who is proud to entertain; very carefully, she cut the cakes with mathematical precision.

"I hope I get a corner with frosting!"

Rae looked serious. "You'll have to take your chances."

"O, there's a bigger piece!"

But Rae, now in charge, served me first. To the gluttons she remarked, "Mind your manners," and this produced giggles. I was on the spot and endeavored, rather unsuccessfully, to behave as if we were "playing house," with Rae the officious hostess bustling about over a punch bowl which contained real champagne punch. O, the Sewing Club, the Bridge Club, the luncheons of my younger days! My very first club: two little girls in caps and aprons, learning to cook. All this was like going back as far as the first tea party, with miniature tea sets and dolls for people.

Willie was glowing, radiant. Almost overnight she had acquired an aura of victory and assurance. The radiance was subdued, more like pearls than diamonds. The old Willie, who was tall, skinny, and uncertain, with the hesitating, tight voice of shyness, now spoke with the voice of love, with more laughter in it. No hard edges. The girls were looking at Willie as if she were an older sister. Getting a man was still regarded in the young feminine set, it appeared, with more awe than getting all A's.

We had all had our cake, and it was getting late. I made my my way out between the lounging, sprawling boys to go into my bedroom. I was tired.

As I undressed, I remembered a student of mine, a boy, who had attempted to define various kinds of girls in a new argot. Of one he liked especially he said, "She is a ningy girl."

"What's a ningy girl? I asked. I was very fond of this boy, who was a talented artist, tall and handsome.

"She is a girl who is out of the giggly stage. A girl is at first giggly, then she is a ningy girl. A ningy girl is a girl who doesn't giggle, but she still complains a lot. She takes quite a bit of managing to make her behave herself. But she is cute. She has possibilities."

"What happens when she is better than a ningy girl?" I asked, feeling that I owed it to my profession to keep up with the current slang.

He almost blushed. "Now you mustn't take this the wrong way. It sounds different from what it means. We call her 'Hot Shit.'"

"What does that mean?"

"It means she is cool and sophisticated and never complains. She is very good-looking and you want to go to bed with her, but she will discriminate, and there is plenty to like about her even if she will not go to bed. She is smooth and exciting."

Now, drawing on my flowered cotton robe, I sighed. Willie was probably still a ningy girl. I had no way of knowing. Or was she "Hot Shit?" In the midst of these rather confusing thoughts, I heard someone screaming out on front campus. Was she being attacked? Was she letting off an excess of energy? I went to my front window and looked out to see Willie buried under autumn leaves, rolling, laughing, and screaming as she came up for air, with a young man doing the tossing under this crackling blanket. Finally she was quiet as Robert (for it could have been no other) sat up, took her in his arms, and gave her a long kiss.

There was Robert, his head a dark silhouette against the lamps beyond; a vigorous head of curly dark hair, long strong arms holding Willie—and, as they drew apart, he stood and pulled Willie to her feet. A beard! Would that be scratchy for kissing? Or sexy and exciting, like the sharp, crackling leaves? Very reluctantly, Robert put his arm around Willie and began to draw her to the front door. I drew my curtains, but I heard murmurs. "Please don't go," Willie said. The deeper voice of Robert. "I don't want to, darling." Silence . . . and finally, the heavy front door closing with a thud.

"When I was in college. . . ." Yes, on the evening of my engagement, I put a candle in my window and was serenaded with a sweetheart song by all the "brothers." Romantic distance. But I remembered a meadow in moonlight and lying there with the man I loved. As clearly as if this happened only a day ago, I saw the mist, the full moon, his face, and felt the joy, the growing. Good grief! I had not thought of this for so many years that I could not count them. The deep-down remembering, the fire coming up in my body, the passion fresh and new, glowing in my belly, my breasts, my lips to my toes—everywhere he touched me.

Were we any better off because we never rolled and tumbled on the earth, never dared to see bodies bare and reap the consequences? The world without clothes (duly studied in the tortuous prose of Thomas Carlyle) was a foreign country full of dangers—and ignorance.

Yet over all these conflicts of my youth lay the sickly sweet romanticism of Keats, Shelley, Mrs. Browning, mixed, curiously enough, with Puritanism and the doctrine of virginity, a real devil's brew for a bad marriage.

Robert and Willie were having *fun*. It was on this evening I realized that whatever they would do about sex was no business of mine; I'm not at all sure I ever got beyond being a ningy girl until I was thirty years old.

Victoria

Time passed almost more swiftly than I could have imagined the year before, when the days dragged for want of strength. A week that seemed like a day had passed when Victoria arrived. Late September varied between Indian summer days and a chill that promised winter. We were having a frosty day when Victoria came from her warm country, Biafra, via New York.

We were now in business. Plumbing was leaking, locks were sticking, maintenance men were cursing.

Rae came to tell me that her roommate was here at last. I went down the hall to welcome her. She was small and very black, with her hair arranged in brushed wings and a soft bun in back. She gave me one of the biggest, brightest smiles I have ever seen.

"How do you do," I said. "I am Mrs. Martin, the house mother." Some ten girls were standing around. I went with Victoria down to her room on the first floor corridor, where she sat on her bed, suddenly looking dazed and tired after the effusive American welcome the girls had given her. She was wearing a beige sweater and skirt and tiny gold earrings.

"I'm almost exhausted after three days in New York," she said. She spoke English beautifully, with a cultured voice and a catch in her throat. "At home I live in such a small village."

"New York is enough to exhaust anyone," I said. "We will leave you alone now to unpack and get your bearings—do please come to me if I can help."

I went back to my room, and when I came out an hour or so later, Rae was sitting in the middle of the hall and said, "I'm disappointed. She is so *quiet*." I wondered if Rae had expected Victoria to arrive in full African regalia, beating on a bongo drum.

"You ought to be ashamed of yourself, you old do-gooder," I said, feeling quite angry with Rae and her relentless stirring things up in an effort to improve society. Now she sat on the floor with her arms around her knees, behaving as if Victoria were a doll she planned to play with.

But having got an unworthy remark off her chest, Rae appeared to rally. She rather likes being scolded, I thought, with surprise.

"Victoria is singing in the bathroom," she acknowledged, as if informing me that in one respect, Victoria was enjoying herself. "She hasn't enough warm clothes," she added irrelevantly. I made a note to ask Miss Sayles, who had engineered the admission of Victoria, to find out what could be obtained at the Thrift Shop at the Episcopal Church.

The next day I went to see Victoria, who was sitting on her bed as if it were the only safe place in the world.

"How are you getting along?" I knew she must be weary of being visited and welcomed to death and gazed upon as if she were a being from another planet. Only dark-skinned Maria greeted her warily, like a well-behaved cat biding its time, but during the noisy hour the previous evening, Maria had made more noise than anyone else, seizing the center of the stage in a fine display of sibling rivalry.

"I'm cold," Victoria volunteered.

"What's it like in your country?"

"Well, the average yearly temperature is 80."

I went out and dug up an old electric blanket, came back

and removed from Victoria's bed the blankets and comforters Rae had piled there until it must have been like sleeping crushed under a small mountain. I was not at all sure that Victoria could accept our clucking concern, but I had not counted on the aristocratic response of receiving graciously. When I explained the workings of the electric blanket, she looked a trifle daunted, but game.

The next morning I found a note under my door addressed in neat handwriting to "Mrs. Martin, Bixby Dorm." It said,

> Dear Mrs. Martin,
> Thank you very much for the blanket.
>   This has been my warmest night since I
> arrived in America.
>
>   Yours,
>   Victoria

Another day passed, and I heard Victoria playing the piano with unself-conscious enjoyment—Mozart! Then there were rumbling African rhythms of native dances. That evening Elizabeth Wyckoff arrived at dinner with a stocking cap of brown, beige and orange she had knitted in one day. I took the cap to the dorm and presented it to Victoria. She began to smile with wonder, and turned the cap over and over in her beautiful hands, admiring its colors and reflecting on the kindness that created it.

"O, I love it. Do give me Mrs. Wyckoff's address so I can call on her. I don't even know who she is!"

"Do you mind if we give you things?" I really did not know how to explain; perhaps my whole youth as a minister's daughter was getting in my way. I bumbled on.

"You don't have to wear things people give you unless you really *like* them. Americans are aware that we have too much and we like to give things." I had a flashing mental image of the piles of food that were carried out from our dining room, and, juxtaposed with this, the TV pictures of starving babies in Biafra, with distended bellies and razor-thin ribs.

Victoria smiled her wide smile. "You needn't be concerned. I love it. People are so gentle with me here. The girls are delightful—they come in just to chat, and they seem so interested." She was being polite, like a duchess at a flower show.

"I would like to talk with you, too; how about coming down to my sitting room?" I felt as if I were talking to someone very old.

When we reached the sitting room, Victoria observed with her large, dark eyes whatever might be called an art object; the small carved lion in ivory, the alabaster globe, the graceful vase from Japan, the paintings—different things from the ones that caught the eyes of Barbie.

We sat in silence for a moment. I felt like an old nanny, and remembered that Victoria's father was chieftain of his tribe.

"Do you find our food difficult to eat?"

"Well, it *is* very bland," she said, with an apologetic look. "I am accustomed to highly spiced food."

"How about pepper?"

"It's all right, but you do not have our spices." She laughed as if she felt she could manage. "I haven't felt homesick yet because everybody is so nice to me. You needn't worry," she said kindly.

I smiled. It suddenly seemed so amusing to have Victoria trying to reassure me! I had never before *lived* with a black person, and now I had two, one the product of an English boarding school, the other a daughter of the ghetto. It occurred to me now that a black bishop from the South had been an overnight guest in our home when I was around twelve. This single small event had for some reason helped me not to view the black race with the prevalent prejudices of my youth; unconsciously, I had responded to the circumstance that this man outranked my father.

But Victoria was waiting for this reverie to pass.

"Can you visit your brothers during vacations?"

"Yes, and I have three brothers over here, you know. One is a doctor in Montreal. And next summer I must find a job in New York." Then wistfully, "Are there any beaches in New York?"

"Oh, yes, lots of them. And maybe you should get a job on Cape Cod." I stopped, wondering. I was quite sure Victoria would not like to be a maid, even if one of the girls had said it was great fun.

"I wonder how you will like the snow, when all the glorious color of the leaves is gone—sometimes it is a mean snow with a north wind, and sometimes it seems like magic when it comes softly in the night."

"Is it slippery? Will I be able to walk on it?"

"Yes, if you are careful, and we get you some good boots, with heavy corrugated soles. I like it—I like waking up to see a different world."

Victoria smiled. I knew she knew the feeling.

"Come along," I said, "it's turning rather cold," for I could see her clasping her arms around herself as if she felt chilly.

We went into the living room, and I knelt before the big fireplace, crushing paper and placing the sticks of kindling carefully; I lit a match, and watched the yellow flames sing up in forked lightning tongues. We sat on the floor and heard the beating wings of the fire, heard the sighing of sap in the wood, smelled the pine and birch, the good acrid smell.

Victoria's face shone in the firelight as the shadows grew grey in the folds of the draperies and a thick dark came down in the tall windows; only the fire was alive and speaking for the next five minutes.

Then she stood up and left me, where I sat, hearing the girls come in and run up the stairs, until time to dress for dinner.

I noticed that Victoria was gradually taking on the nightly habits of the dorm population, with one exception; at night she braided her hair in a number of tight little pigtails, each one tied with a narrow yellow ribbon. She bounded about in a cotton print nightgown from Africa and a bright yellow quilted robe from America, with all the little pigtails sticking straight up—a pickaninny hair-do.

"Did you keep warm today?" I asked her. For it was turning quite cold and I heard the skittering of mice in the walls at night.

"Well, not exactly, but I have a coat and the cap and Rae's mittens and boots. My nose didn't run."

She was a beam of warmth from a hot country.

"May I see the coat?" In spite of myself, I was being maternal. We went to her room and I inspected the coat. It was a fine heavy grey coat made in England of llama cloth—a treasure from the Thrift Shop?

"Very nice," I said, feeling the texture. "The weather man says it will snow over the weekend. I hope it will be fluffy and come down like feathers." I sat down on her bed.

I was feeling rather morose, having just concluded a conversation on the subject of pot with some girls who either left the room or dodged the whole issue by brightly introducing other topics.

"Do you have pot in Biafra?"

She laughed as if this was a foolish question. "Oh, yes. The soldiers smoke it all the time. We have all sorts of drugs." She was beginning to open up and talked much more freely. I felt a sense of relief to talk about Biafra for a change; the urge for social reform always seems more comfortable when it is not too close to the bone.

"Where is Rae? I said.

"Oh, she is out at a meeting about getting more blacks on campus. I think everyone here makes a silly fuss about race. At home I read so much about it that I thought I would have trouble here, and I don't. And in New York I saw lots of black people mingling with white people everywhere."

"You don't get the picture yet," I said, wondering if she knew the extent of our guilt over slavery. "Did you see Harlem?"

"No, but I will at the holidays. But in Africa it is *different*."

I gave it up. It struck me as ironical that Victoria imagined race was all right in America. I winced as I thought about her meeting with her first snub, or worse. Wadleigh College was over-protection.

Victoria had stretched out on Rae's bed, but now she got up and ran over to her dresser, where she had the family pictures standing among the usual clutter of cosmetics to be seen on every girl's dresser. I looked around at the bright blue and yellow colors Rae had brought from home for spreads and draperies.

Victoria held out a picture. "We have a very big stone house, like an English house."

"Is it inside Biafra?"

"Oh, yes. It was fifteen miles from the firing line, and all day and all night we could hear the guns, all kinds of guns, machine guns, rifles, bombs, going off constantly."

Her face had turned sad, almost pathetic, but she spoke with absolute poise. "The outside of the house was damaged by bullets and explosions."

"Is it like an English manor house?"

"Yes, I think so. *Very* big. And all the other houses in the village are small."

I wondered what Victoria would think of a small suburban home with wall-to-wall carpeting. "I'm glad you are living in a big house now," I said rather lamely.

But she wanted to show me a picture of her father in his chieftain's robe and hat, holding a large thing that looked something like a sceptre. He looked very distinguished, like one of my own people dressed in the ceremonial robes of a fraternal order.

"What is the name of the tribe?"

"Ubiobiobi. My father went to Iowa State."

"I'm glad you have brothers in this country."

"Yes. One is getting a Ph.D. at Michigan State."

Now I understood even better why she and Maria had not much in common, for Maria had struggled up from poverty; she had told me her mother was a cleaning woman and her father a laborer out of work. A point for Wadleigh—scholarships for both of these girls who needed them.

I sat fascinated by the picture of the chief in his official robes, the old and the new coming together, much as a New England board of selectmen exists in the midst of the vast political machine which has evolved at a federal level.

"Are your parents in the house now?"

"Yes." Victoria sat down by her desk, which she was using as a proper desk with all her books and papers stacked on it. It had amused me to see the other girls sitting on the floor when they studied, while a glance into Rae's and Victoria's room

63

revealed Victoria's back as she sat up straight at her desk the way we used to do.

"But for a while we had to go away and hide in a tiny village in a hut. My father was against the war, and his life was in danger. Lots of sensible people in Biafra were against the war. But now things are better because of help from the Red Cross and other people who came to help us. After we lived in the village, we had to go away and hide in the bush."

My mind boggled at what she had been through, this little girl with the big smile, the singing voice I heard in the halls.

She went on, "Americans *talk* about war. I have been so terrified and now I feel safe in America, and I cannot talk or say what I feel about war."

I was praying that no one would come into the room. I asked Victoria one more question.

"Where were the starving people we saw on TV?"

She smiled, but with a great sadness in her eyes.

"Everywhere. They were with us in the village. They were in every village." She had tears in her eyes now.

I could not ask her if she knew what it was to fear starvation—of course she knew.

She turned and showed me more pictures. Her mother was there with the children, dressed sometimes in long flowing African prints, other times in tailored European dress. There was a christening at a high Anglican church, with the tiny black baby in a conventional long white dress and bonnet, and the relatives standing around with pride. There was a portrait of the whole family, an African version of a Victorian portrait.

"My mother says she would not have had so many children, but she wanted a girl, and she went on until she got one."

"By the way, what is your other name?"

"Eno. It means 'gift from God.' I was born with a strange hollow in my forehead, and my parents thought it made me special—now I don't have it any more."

It was my turn to feel tears starting in my eyes. "You are still special." I took Victoria's hand. "Come on down to my sitting room and I'll show you a picture of my mother."

When we were settled on the love seat, I showed her my

mother, circa 1909, dressed in a long gown of coffee-colored broadcloth, with a high lace collar and lace sleeves; the dress was embroidered with brown soutache braid in swirls down the side panels. Her abundant hair was piled on top of her head with soft bangs and tendrils in front.

Victoria examined the picture with loving care. "She looks like one of the English queens." With a start, I realized this was so. I was one year old at this time; now the Victorian and Edwardian periods were generations away. I had known rather well four generations of my family: my parents, my siblings, my children, and my grandchildren.

After this moving moment, we said good night and Victoria ran down the hall singing, with all the exuberance of a little girl who has been good to the old folks.

A freshman was sitting in the hall by the desk where every evening someone took the duty for the telephone; the usual complement of boys was waiting. I told the freshman, a soft and gentle girl called Buffy, about Victoria's house.

"Yes, and she had servants who laid out her clothes and everything," Buffy said, and went back to her books.

I was really "shook up." I went into my bedroom and thought about the differences between the African aristocrat and the inheritor of American slavery. Would Victoria, who knew about civil war with her own people, be able to understand the black militants of our country and the reasons for their revolt? I would have to know her better before I dared to ask.

As the month turned toward Hallowe'en, I explained to Victoria that Hallowe'en began with All Hallows, when the ghosts of the saints were supposed to rise from their graves and walk, getting ready for All Saints' Day on November 1. She understood this immediately.

"Then this turned into witches, black cats, goblins, scarecrows," I continued.

Victoria grinned. "Maybe people like bad better than good for having fun."

"Well, no, if you consider Christmas—oh, I don't know."

She might be right. "We have certainly managed to make Christmas less holy. Anyway, the children get dressed up in costumes and masks and go around the neighborhood saying, 'Trick or treat!' And if they don't get a treat, like candy or apples, they play a trick." But I could not tell Victoria about the threats of bombs on Hallowe'en, or the little black boy in Detroit who died from heroin put in his candy. Only five years old! Pure evil, not make-believe.

Victoria understood. Apparently the voodoos and charms of her native land had something in common with our ghosts and goblins.

The weekend before Hallowe'en, we had two little girls visiting us. They were both nine years old. One was Chinese with long black silky hair; the other was from a poor white family in our own state. They had spent six weeks last summer at Wadleigh Lodge, a camp on property the college owned by the lake, where our students took care of a group of under-privileged children every summer. All the little girls came back on the weekend before Hallowe'en for a visit with the girls who had been their counselors. There were twenty-five of them on campus.

Rae asked, "May I please take two of the living room couch cushions for the little girls to sleep on? They mustn't sleep on the floor without a mattress." She looked as anxious as any worried mother.

"Ask Barbie—I'm almost sure she will say yes, if you put the cushions back in the morning."

The little girls were ecstatic at having so much sisterly attention from big, rangy counselors. At ten that night noisy hour came on as usual, and the uneasy clumping hours of study exploded with ringing screams and curses, clankings from the Coke machine, and record players blasting rock. It was a fine catharsis, and I only wished I could join the group rolling in athletic anguish on the hall carpet to the exercising record, "Chicken Fat." These girls looked uncommonly thin to me, but they were all bent on becoming thinner. Leslie was eating nothing now but hot dogs, and Barbie, who led the pack, nothing but grapefruit.

Rae came along to say they were having a birthday party for Victoria in Pat and Melinda's room, and would I come? I picked my way through the weight blasters, barely missing outflung arms, and then managed not to collide with three girls racing to answer the telephone as I walked down the corridor.

Pat, a tall girl who walked like a ballet dancer, was stuffing her long legs into a pair of clean wrinkled pants. Freshly washed clothes were piled on the bed.

"What on earth are you doing?" I asked idiotically.

"I want to see if they have shrunk."

Melinda, a brain surgeon's daughter from Boston, sat on the floor with her long legs crossed, smiling in a secret way she had, as if everyone was crazy but she loved them all anyway. She was six feet tall and had told me she was going to be a surgical nurse. Pat and Melinda were neat and "square," but they got along well with the others, with a minimum of cattishness.

The two little girls and Rae stood in the middle of the room with a chocolate cake on a trunk between them; a few pink and white candles stood up bravely to say "Happy Birthday." Willie, who lived next door, sat on a bed near the window, looking like a contented Siamese cat who had stood mewing, but was now content. I had observed on Willie's door a mysterious message, ripped (to my horror) from the flyleaf of a book, which said, "To My Father."

When Rae lit the candles and everyone sang with zest, the two little girls stood at rapt attention, their faces glowing, and not looking in the least deprived. Then Rae ran across the hall and came back with Victoria, who was now wearing a long African skirt of brown print, a wraparound blouse, and a beige filmy scarf on her head.

Victoria sat down on the other bed with stunned surprise, and her deep velvety black eyes gazed on the little girls as if what she had missed most was children. Then she carefully put her finger under each side of her glasses and wiped a single tear from each eye.

When she had blown out the candles, we each had a piece of cake about two by two inches, and Melinda said to Victoria, "Were you surprised?"

"I am in another world," Victoria said, looking at the little girls.

This was all I learned of Victoria in the fall, but later, in January, I came in one afternoon and found her reading the *New York Times* and taking notes. Subject: the Vietnam War. Very often our *New York Times* was not even unfolded. Victoria had by now gone into slacks which were combined with a vest of African print over a red blouse.

"They had better get tough with North Vietnam," she said. "Those guys are *mean* and it's true they will massacre everyone who doesn't agree with them, if they win." Victoria projected on Vietnam her war experiences, and I didn't know then, nor do I now, whether she was right. But "those guys"! She was picking up our slang very fast.

"I wish you would talk to the girls about the war," I said.

"No matter how much you read about it and see it on TV, you can't imagine how horrible it is," she said furiously.

"Why don't you try to tell us all you can?"

She shook her head, but managed to look more agreeable. "The trouble with American kids is that they are so idealistic and go around *talking* all the time about the poor and war and peace, but they believe every single thing anyone tells them—they don't know what they are doing."

"Some of them are doing quite a lot," I said gently.

She went back to reading the paper.

"Aren't you going to dinner?"

"It's too early." Victoria had starved enough so she could go without food any time she felt like it; she was not to be budged by suggestions.

It was never more moving to know Victoria than one evening in January when she came to my bedroom door and asked if she might watch the eleven o'clock news in my sitting room in the hope of hearing something about the ending of the war in Biafra. She was shining in that dark, beautiful way she

68

had, a glow such as one might see in a satiny black pearl, and she said, "I am so glad it is over, so glad, I don't even care that we lost—war is so terrible."

"Of course you may watch—may I join you? Are you afraid of massacres, of retributions?"

"No." I was surprised at this answer. I put on my robe and we crossed the hall together. Victoria sat on the love seat. She was dressed in pale yellow flannel sleeping culottes with a low neck. She had given over her little pigtails and had her hair in pink rollers. Her small breasts drooped under her soft culotte in exactly the same way we have seen in portraits of naked African women. Hair rollers! I had a fleeting impression of how we used to put in water-wave combs and steam our hair over the spout of a tea kettle.

Together we watched the Nigerian representative at the United Nations utter a solemn statement on the surrender of the Biafran people, together with an assurance that no one would be molested. All were urged to return to their homes.

"Mr. Uloh," Victoria said, and her voice rolled the familiar name as if it gave her pleasure.

We saw the great dry landscape of Biafra, and some pictures of starving children; one was of a mother trying to put a bit of soft food into the mouth of a shriveled baby, who was too weak to accept it.

Then Victoria became suffused with anger. She raised her voice and cried, "All the food you sent us—I never saw a bit of it given to the people! It was all given to the soldiers so they could fight. It was wrong, all wrong, the whole thing. It was all done by the military, and we know they were wrong, and God is punishing us for ever revolting when we should not have done it."

"I don't think God had anything to do with it, Victoria," I said.

But Victoria was too enraged, too distraught, to listen to a remark like that from someone who did not know what war is like: the bombs, the frantic running, the fear, the hunger.

"Now we have lost everything—education, our culture, our pride, and we should not have done it. We will be put back many years. We fought our own brothers and we will suffer for it."

I thought of our own South, and of my Quaker grandfather in the Union Army hauling medical supplies on a mule; his letter on the bloody battle of Murfreesboro—his horror at the wounded and the dead lying in pouring rain. I thought of my own divided inheritance, the Breckenridges of Kentucky and their slaves, the Quakers in Illinois who were helping the slaves to escape through the underground. "We fought our own brothers." And we are suffering for it.

"Those military men should be tried and punished," Victoria cried out. Her voice was rising higher in her anguish. "They hung a woman in the streets—I saw it. First they stripped her naked and dragged her in the public streets, because she did not approve of the war. And they raped women, and they threw dissidents into prison. Those were not Nigerians—those were our own officers, our own warmongers. Now they will all be granted amnesty—they will not be punished."

"Abraham Lincoln did not believe we should punish the South," I said. But Victoria did not see any connection (and perhaps there was none), or perhaps she was too wild with sorrow to hear.

"And let me tell you about my brother. He wrote a letter to Lagos, where he had been in college, because he wanted to know how his friends were, and they threw him in jail for *that*. He would not tell them anything because they would have taken my father also."

Now she was yelling and sobbing. She rocked back and forth and held her face in her hands. "We have lost everything, everything, and we deserve it. All the educated people in Biafra knew we could not win; we knew we should be one country, united."

"Maybe you will go back there and do your bit, be a teacher?"

"I certainly will." This thought seemed to soothe her.

"I just wish they had shown more pictures," she said, in simple homesickness, and went out with tears on her cheeks.

I sat there, stunned and dumb, thinking about her pride, her

70

graciousness, her sense of *noblesse oblige*. In our cold white world of a New England winter Victoria was learning to be at home, even if she missed her dry, hot climate and the damp gloom of the rain forest, her mother and father, and being with her people at this crucial time. But she was game; she did not plan to go home until her education was finished, until she had prepared herself to help her country, even if it took years.

Late in the spring, I opened the local paper and saw that Victoria had been out addressing the local Lions' Club. The headline blared, "Wadleigh Student from Biafra Tells of Ducking Shots in Brush." Her face beamed out in a photograph, round and amused, with her bone-rimmed glasses giving her a scholarly look. She was decked out in earrings and beads.

"You are all so gullible," Victoria announced to the Lions, whom I could picture sitting there after their big satisfying lunch, smoking cigars and feeling indulgent toward this little black foreigner. "American news about the war came largely from press handouts from the warring sides, not from journalists on the scene . . . it was mostly our fault . . . we learned our lesson.

"I wish you would be more critical about what you believe. We are doing the same thing you have done—technology and pollution are ruining your country and they are starting to ruin ours. I want to stop this in my country. My happiness will not be in a house or three cars; it will be in finding balance within myself."

Waxing humorous, Victoria told them she had expected to see crime, cowboys, sneakers, and blue jeans in America.

"Don't generalize about other countries. I've only seen lions before today in a zoo!"

I wondered if the Lions sat up and took notice. Could they possibly have walked out a bit jolted? "You are just as uninformed about us as we were uninformed about you," Victoria concluded.

I felt like cheering. Victoria, before the year was over, had changed from a polite girl, shy but angry, into a woman who knew what she thought and was not afraid to say so.

Interlude

But in telling Victoria's story I'm ahead of myself; as autumn moved toward winter, the action in the dorm became more intense, and my inner life began to grow toward a renewed acceptance and appreciation.

October came with tapestries of color spread over the hills and the campus covered in red, pink, gold, lemon. Every time I walked out on the campus, breathing in the crisp air, I felt intoxicated with colors like wine. On rainy days, the leaves dripped water colors; on days of burning blue skies, they glowed, more beautiful than stained glass in the sun.

I was still avoiding the adults on campus except at dinner, when I felt I had to be with them by necessity. I do not like large crowds or shouting at meals; moreover, I had a private conviction that the first year in a strange place is a time to proceed with caution. But now something happened; my own daughter, who was then thirty-six, decided to visit me, flying all the way from California. She had never seen New England—and she had taken a year off from her own teaching after a rugged time of producing three children without, as it were, dropping the teaching permanently. Her husband, who was one of my favorite people, felt he could manage alone for a week.

Everything came together when Alberta arrived, vivid and joyous even after being stuck in the Sumner Tunnel in Boston for thirty minutes in a taxi, thus missing her bus to New Devon. As always, she brought me a fresh surging of energy. What a week that was! Elizabeth gave Alby her apartment across the street from the campus; Miss Sayles, Victoria's sponsor, offered her own home for an adult party; and finally, the girls wanted to give Alby a party in our big living room. They did this with real style. No one forgot to light the candles or build the fire or order the little sandwiches and cakes and coffee. Everyone was a model of decorum; a muted and courteous atmosphere prevailed.

And every day we drove together through the blazing color of the countryside, went out for lunch the way we did sometimes before she married, and we talked. I remembered Alby; no one could howl more vigorously when things went wrong; no one could praise more generously when things were right. I had felt she had never quite forgiven me for going so far away, but as we said goodbye, she put her arms around me and remarked gently, "I can feel this is the right place for you." She did not criticize; she did not condescend. To this day, I have a lump in my throat when I say goodbye to my daughter or my son. For a moment I could not speak.

"I've had a glorious time," Alby said, as she climbed on the Boston bus. "You look so *well!*"

"See you at Christmas!" We waved as the bus pulled out. I felt healthier, less cautious, more like an insider, and very much as if my daughter saw me as a *person.* Grown-up children can give one a real "high." What happened? We crossed a bridge together.

And was I changing? My mother said at age seventy-five, "No human being ever changes. Look at your father." Yet he balanced in her as a tree in earth.

I was finding out that the place where the "brook and river meet" was not serene; it became a rushing torrent that invaded my rooms and the hall rather frequently. I had conferences with

Barbie and enjoyed my morning talks with Mrs. Perley, who said, "Girls will be girls," and smiled.

On the morning of October 31, I lay on the cot in my studio and looked at the intestines of pipes on the ceiling. The steam was rumbling and hissing in the old radiator. Yes, I was changing; I was being forced out of old attitudes into a world so full of life and energy so demanding, that I was being renewed out of sheer necessity to go on living in it.

If, in the past, I had made the rules in the classroom: "You may not haul up the Venetian blinds and break the cords. You may not invade my desk, look at other students' work, interrupt, or take other students' books. . . . You may feel free to speak out on any of your ideas"—all of this was physical control aimed at mental freedom. Or at home, "Do pick up your dirty clothes and put them in the laundry basket, do say 'excuse me,' do *not* sit and read with your legs hanging over a chair arm when I have guests"—all this the oft-repeated, mechanical imploring of a beleaguered mother trying for good manners.

I wrote in my journal, "Only two months here, and day by day everything is going deeper and deeper. It's a great ego trip. I am treated like someone special, a grandma. What goes on behind my back, upstairs, or when I'm asleep, is still rather a mystery. Mary Barnes says the rumor is that they are going to 'do away with house mothers.' If so, I am living at the end of an era. I receive more attention than an only child; my clothes are remarked upon, 'Wow, a black dress—really cool, like the city.' Or, 'It's O.K. for older ladies to wear lipstick, but not *too* much.'

"Whether they hear me or not, I have no idea. Lord! All I do is *listen*."

It was quiet in the studio. *Adagio*, part of Vivaldi's *The Seasons*, the autumn leaves fallen, brown, swept up into bonfires, the smell of leaves burning, the turning toward winter so far from spring, the deeper and deeper time when I wanted to hibernate with my acorns gathered, like a chipmunk, down in a hollow. Down to what? Learning about what?

"My considered opinion," (I wrote grumpily) "is that most of these girls have an emotional age ranging from fourteen to twenty-five. Everything is 'cool,' they say, but everything they

74

do is *hot*, except studying. Women's Libbers should have a sight of them when the phone rings. Bedlam! Passion! A real old panting, squealing fit at the anticipation of the sound of the male voice. Or, dejected, coming out afterwards, 'It was only mother. *Shit!'"*

My journal was in contrast to my outward behavior; I was "hanging in there" with all the aplomb of a lightweight boxer who had no idea of when the K.O. might come, but I was learning to deliver punches and becoming less the invisible woman all the time.

Ghosts and Goblins

Hallowe'en came and went. In the afternoon, some of us carved jack-o-lanterns. The house was redolent of burned pumpkin when we lit candles behind the (perhaps revealing) masks.

Rae, thin and stooped, came in while this was going on, grabbed a knife and began hacking away at a small pumpkin, sitting on the floor and dumping seeds and pulp on an old newspaper. When she had finished her carving and her creation sat gleaming on the harvest table in the hall, she looked at it as if it were part of herself that delighted her.

"I never carved a pumpkin before," she said. How could that be? When evening came, Rae spent most of her time admiring her pumpkin, which had a toothy, mournful look. At intervals she would exclaim, "I love the smell of it!"

The pumpkins were masks of Comedy and Tragedy. An art major carved a rakish one which beamed out with an authentic mixture of evil and jollity. Orange candles burned on the living room mantel. The moon was proclaiming fire and light and color that evening; would we be "spooked"?

76

Early evening was not exciting. We had an invasion of little boys who threw red and blue paint on our windows and fermented cider on our doors, then squirted shaving cream on one girl's suede coat as she was running across campus. By ten o'clock we had survived four big bumbling high school boys who said they wanted something to eat, and were mollified by candies from our "Trick or Treat" punch bowl. From my sitting room, I kept hearing the sounds of feet running and voices giggling, so I put down my book and went out to investigate. Where was everybody? No boys. Probably everyone who wasn't studying was up at Dartmouth or somewhere raising the Old Nick.

Les and Lisa were sitting on the living room floor with their mutual boy friend, Jeff, playing with Tinker Toys. I was never quite ready for these abrupt returns to childhood. Until then, I had seen Les as a messy adolescent and Lisa as a stringy girl who spoke in a nasal voice and sang in unbearable tones.

"Well, this proves that old people have dirty old minds," I said. I was glad they were not out smoking pot, and even more glad they were not busy getting drunk.

Lisa said in an imploring little-girl voice, "Can't we carve the big pumpkin, *please?*"

I looked at Lisa in astonishment. Was this the same Lisa who entered the house each time with a loud nasal proclamation of wrath, especially when the mail came late in the morning? My impressions of Lisa had been confined to envy for anyone who could be so vocal about injustice-collecting. She would stand in the middle of the hall when she got a letter from her mother, yelling, "Listen to this! God, isn't she awful?" And Lisa was the great impersonator; she could imitate every one of us. When she imitated me, she became a tired lady in a bathrobe, who walked in and said with contained lady-like grieving, "I can't sleep—please tone it down a little, girls."

And Lisa, in her own image, was not inhibited. She could sit on the bench by my door and announce to anyone within hearing distance that she had a wild time on her Saturday night date. "I hardly knew this guy, and he tried to unzip my pants. God!"

All these thoughts were delaying my answer. "Yes, take over the big pumpkin." I got knives and newspapers. The big pumpkin was sitting on the baby grand piano. I went back to my reading, and quiet prevailed for an hour and a half, precisely the way it used to do when my children had found a really good project. At such times, I found the quiet held dangers, and when I reached the peak of curiosity required, I would go to see "what was going on."

I went out, and found that Jeff had carved the greatest pumpkin of all; it had round eyes and a wide curved mouth that went up on one side like a tipsy recumbent comma. Les was squashing her hands through the pumpkin pulp and seeds and letting this gooey mess drip through her fingers.

"It feels like being at the beach and squashing the wet sand, only it is quicksand and you go down in it and can't get out unless you *drag* yourself out."

They got up. Jeff peered through his hair, which hung over his wan face, and then through tinted glasses with steel frames. His expression, what I could see of it, seemed appropriate to an English vicar in charge of a nursery.

Lisa said, "Can Jeff go upstairs and put our pumpkin out on the ledge over the front door?"

"Yes, if he comes back down," I said with irony.

Jeff laughed. "What do you think I'm going to do—stay up there all night?"

"It wouldn't surprise me."

Back to my book, until I heard screams and the sound of the front door slamming. I wrapped a coat around me and went out into the bitter cold night. All three of them were dancing around in their bare feet and yelling with joy. Above the big front door the pumpkin beamed its fire with regal majesty. The three temporary children were wild with delight.

"Isn't it *marvelous?*" they screamed.

For about two hours after this, the house was so quiet that I thought Hallowe'en was over. Then I went down the corridor to check the thermostat, which I found was turned up to 80.

Lisa, in the hall, was breathless. "We went out to the graveyard, and I kept hanging on to Jeff's sleeve, and he said,

'Let go of me,' but I heard something in the bushes and I was scared to death."

Was this story only to divert me? For at 1:05 in the morning they signed out to spend the night with Jeff at his fraternity house. They would pretend they didn't know, being freshmen, that it was illegal to sign out for an overnight after twelve midnight. I sighed and went back to bed, knowing that Barbie would check the book. Hallowe'en was over.

But the ghouls and goblins were still busy. At 2:20 I woke up and realized someone had come in and turned up the heat again, enveloping all those of us who were sleeping in a steam bath. I was suffocating, and got up to remedy this.

In the hall I found a freshman named Phyllis, also Melinda (who was in a short nightgown with a large head of hair rollers topped by a cap big enough for a Neanderthal woman), and Les, all looking scared.

It was like Act II in a bad play. Heightening of tensions for contrast—further involvement of characters. Audience supposed to be on tenterhooks. I was too tired to think. Peering around through the entry, I saw Lisa hunched up on the floor, making out another overnight slip.

She got up. "I am going away," she announced, "and I am not coming back." She was barefoot and bedraggled.

"Don't you want your shoes?" Les said in the tone of a distressed mother.

"No, I do not." But Lisa came and sat down by the front hall desk. "No one likes me in this place so I am going to leave." Beer or pot or what? I asked myself. But something had happened.

Phyllis peeped out at Lisa as I took the overnight slip. It said, for "Time of Return," "No Return," and gave no address. The point of no return; the writing was jagged and I knew almost certainly that Lisa was drunk or stoned.

Phyllis whispered to me, "She was talking on the phone and Pat told her to be quiet, and she called Pat such a filthy name that I can't tell it to you."

I went back to Lisa. She was rattling on incoherently about how no one liked her—she was like someone on a window ledge.

"Please don't go now," I said. "You belong to us, and if you go now, we won't have any chance to help, and you will have an awful time. Maybe your feet will freeze. Where will you go?"

Phyllis, looking round and rosy, came closer and said, "Smile. Please try now, smile just a *little* bit." God in heaven, I thought, Smile buttons! But Lisa did not smile. The silence became oppressive and we stood there wordless, looking at Lisa, hoping she would feel that we cared. In the silence the break came with the click that happens inside; Les felt it and said, "Come on upstairs." Lisa got up and followed along obediently as a child, and I went back to bed.

Two nights later, Lisa was asking to see me, but she wouldn't come without Les. Pat, the faithful messenger, brought this information, went off and came back to say they could come at once. Soon they both came in and sat before me on the love seat, two thin girls whose faces had turned old and solemn. Could they really have played with Tinker Toys, visited the graveyard? Could Lisa have tried to pull the running away stunt? A sense of soap opera washed over me, sudsy stuff, clogging the drains.

Lisa launched into the theme of her mother. The mother-hatred is one of the most frightening things of our time—mother in my day was almost universally honored as the one who, after all, gave one life through birth even if she had her faults; now she has become all too often the scapegoat for everything. Sometimes this seems to me as hypocritical—and extreme—as the former adoration, and weirdly based on revenge, hostility in the midst of love. If I had realized fifty years ago that this would come to be the fashion , would I have dared to have any children? In my youth, I never heard anyone say she or he hated their mother (even if they did) or blame her bitterly for all their shortcomings, for an infantilism carried into adulthood. It takes a really sick person to wish he had never been born, an almost inescapable conclusion from this line of reasoning, although wishing one had been born to someone else might be acceptable—how confusing! If the latter, one would be an entirely different person.

80

Even Ethel Waters, whose mother in early puberty bore her into a world of prostitutes and pimps, wrote movingly of her joy when her mother finally accepted her. For her mother she had only a mature compassion.

Lisa was saying, "I like my step-father, and my own father, too. But *she* never listens to me. She says I talk all the time and never say anything." Possibly true. I had a guilty pang, for I had not been listening, being quite familiar with Lisa's remarks about mother.

"The last time I went home, she said, 'Every time I see you, you look worse.' And when I let my hair grow, she said, 'I'm glad you have decided to be a girl.' You ought to see her in a cocktail dress. She looks like a lady wrestler."

Lisa got her long, bony frame off the love seat and began to imitate her mother bent over the supine frame of a friend named Oscar who had collapsed on the floor at a cocktail party.

"She bent over like this," and Lisa hoisted her arms into a fair likeness of hefty elbows on wide hips, "and yelled, 'Oscar, get up! What's the matter with you, Oscar?'"

For an instant, I saw the redoubtable Mrs. Binks in all her heaviness of mind and body, with her skirt up in back and her elbows akimbo.

Enough of this. "Get to the point," I said. "I already know about your mother. Do you think no one listens to you because she doesn't?"

"Yes. No one except Les." Les was listening carefully, and now she pushed her hair over her ears. Les had the longest hair in the dorm—I think she could sit on it.

Lisa began to cry. "I cry an awful lot."

"But we didn't know that. You never let us see you cry. You always act hard and tough and no one knows you are hurting. You don't let us *know* you are hurt."

"I just wanted to go somewhere, I didn't care where."

"You were running away. I've seen people like you sprawled all over sidewalks in the Haight-Ashbury in San Francisco, completely stoned, and they haven't any place else to run to, except the Pacific Ocean, where some of them end up, swept out to sea."

This was a lucky shot. Lisa's face turned defenseless and solemn, old. We sat for a few minutes, and I tried to sort out in my mind the big pumpkin, the graveyard, the fraternity house—that must have been it, something at the fraternity house—but what? Jeff was a gentle soul who treated both Les and Lisa like sisters, playmates.

I'm *thinking* more this year," Lisa said. She was trying to get off the hook. A few tears slid down the old face.

"Great—but you weren't thinking when you wanted to go out and see the world without any shoes on a freezing night. Why don't you stop pretending to be so tough? Now you are crying and you look vulnerable and soft. And it isn't fair to think that because your mother never listens, no one else does. Because some people besides Les *are* listening."

"I'm worried about my little brother."

Oh, Lord. Conversation with a kid in trouble had no continuity, I thought. And I didn't know how to be subtle, indirect. We were just leaping from one morass into another—playing hop-scotch on the beach, with waves washing over it.

Les decided to change the subject. "Jeff and Lisa and I go around together because I like Jeff in a way that he doesn't feel about me, but he likes us both, so Lisa goes along." (*Like*, that word used today so ambiguously!) "And we aren't going home for Thanksgiving; we are all going away together."

"Where?

"We don't know. Jeff is only a friend, but I like him more than a friend. And Lisa likes Larry. So we went over to see Larry but it was a mess. Lisa had thought she couldn't get anywhere with Larry, so she had fixed Angie up with Larry because Larry doesn't seem to like Lisa."

I felt as if I were being tossed around in a blanket with all these *likes* turning into hearts, flowers, and daggers.

"Dear God," I said with feeling. "Remember I am only a mixed-up old lady and you are making me worse."

Lisa looked desperate, and she was clenching her hands and winding her fingers in and out. It was enough to make me expect a dramatic announcement.

"I just can't stand it," Lisa said in a weepy voice I had never heard from her before. "When I asked Angie if Larry had kissed her, she said, 'Of *course* he has kissed me,' and he never kissed *me*."

Unbelievable, that for this she was ready to run away. The rejected child, the rejected lover. No more hop-scotch. I softened.

Hmmm. *Noli me tangere.* I couldn't put my arms around her or take her on my lap. "How about not going over there for awhile? You are really asking for more pain, you dimwit."

"O.K I guess I will call a guy I know at Williams." The atmosphere had become more lighthearted, and I had forgotten to ask her about the filthy name she called Pat. Just as well, perhaps.

There was a knock at the door. A head poked in and said, "Three people want to know if they can come in and watch your TV."

"What do they want to watch?"

"The 'Carpetbaggers.'"

"Well, it's a vile movie, but come on in," I said, doing some scapegoating myself. Les, Lisa and I went out, and the TV watchers came in. Suddenly Les and Lisa became quite frivolous. Act III had turned into a comedy.

WINTER

Gloom in November

Dank, dour November, with the earth turned to mud and the skies a uniform grey—unremitting rain, soggy and drenching. We sloshed in puddles and the dead leaves stuck to our boots. It was at this time we began to have stealing problems. I often heard that records and cigarettes were being "borrowed" and not returned. A dean at Dartmouth said in public that stealing was the number one problem on every campus in the country, surpassing drugs.

I wondered about the girls' philosophy of "sharing everything," with no distinctions made on the subject of property rights. They were concocting schemes for hiding their money in zipped-up pillow covers, shoes, sanitary napkins, hatboxes, and books, with all the zeal of old ladies on an ocean cruise.

Mid-terms, another cause for gloom. Every night now, girls were curled up studying or typing on the living room floor, with their slippered or bare feet tucked under bathrobes of zany colors. It was hard for me to imagine that it was easier to type on the floor, but there they were, like a bevy of Japanese maidens hard at work.

87

Sometimes Barbie sighed, "Our room is just like open house all the time!" House meetings produced no information on stealing.

One evening Pat appeared at my door and said quietly, "Becky's grandfather has just died and I am in there with her." Becky was a girl to whom I had taken a physical distaste when she sat with her back to me during a TV show, always knitting. I found my reactions irrational, and had tried to subdue them.

Feeling ashamed of myself now, I got up quickly and went down the hall with Pat, who walked swiftly in her long checked robe, looking serious. We found Becky, who was ordinarily stony, looking scared. I found it as difficult as ever to speak about death, but I took her hand and said, "I'm sorry."

We sat helplessly. "Was he very old?" I said.

"Yes, about sixty-two," Becky said through her tears.

My contemporary.

"He had a stroke and he has been in a nursing home for a long time."

"Are you going home?"

"My parents said they would send me the money, but I don't want to go."

There was something odd about Becky, but I could not fathom it and this did not seem the time to wonder. I had a strange feeling she was expressing some pent-up sorrow and felt alone with it.

I said, "Let me know if I can help you, Becky," and went out to the living room where I sat when I wanted to find out what was going on. The girls gave me curious looks. It was very quiet, and two boys sitting on the hall bench behaved as if they were set for the duration.

Eve Leggett, who was always called Legs (doubtless because hers could not have been surpassed by the Mother-of-Us-All in the Garden of Eden), was one of the girls sitting on the floor; she got up and began talking to me in a rushed flutter of exclamations.

"Come into my room," I said, and walked out with Legs following. I took her into my bedroom, and she sat in the easy chair and I stretched out on my bed. I had by this time given up on formalities when privacy was essential.

88

"Becky is pregnant," Legs said, "and after she found it out she went over to the infirmary and asked for some birth control pills, and Dr. James took a test and said, 'It's too late for that, kiddo,' And then she went over to a fraternity house up in a town I won't tell you and got so drunk that she says she did not know what was going on, and four boys raped her. And it was Jeff's fraternity house (O, I didn't mean to tell you) and Jeff tried to stop them, but they just said, 'We want our fair share.' And she didn't even *react* the next day. Really spooky."

My flesh crawled. The dean said pregnancy was a medical problem and we were not to behave as if it were a social problem, but I had to admit that letting four boys rape one is a rather unusual way of meeting a biological emergency.

"How far along is she?" The room, all of a sudden, had an ambience of murk, with the rain pouring down on the dark windows.

"About three months." Legs jumped up and ran off, leaving me in a shambles. I could hear yells from the Butt.

Pat came along next, Nurse Jane Fuzzy-Wuzzy. She sat down, wearing an expression of solicitude. "Becky wants to tell you something because she needs you on her side."

"I already know." I was still shaking. "And I am always on your side. But I am very concerned."

Pat looked glum. "She says she wants to have the baby, and she called her boy friend, and he said he loved her. Pooh." Pat turned up her nose in disgust. "And she told her mother, but now with a death in the family, it was just too much for her mother— and her mother said not to tell her father. And you know what? Some kids are just *sluts*." She named names.

"Oh, dear," I said helplessly. "Well, the question is, is she ready to have a baby and bring it up? Because wanting a baby means someone will have to support her and the baby—and a baby is not a live doll—it grows up."

Pat got down on the floor and sat wringing her hands.

"Sunday night it was really a mess around here. Lisa had an awful week and she was in our room crying, and then we had Becky, and Melinda said, 'What is the matter with me? I haven't got any problems' and I said, 'I love you for that, Mellie.'"

Then Pat got up and walked out, and I lay on my bed with nothing to say. I felt like the old woman who lived in a shoe, with holes in the sole and the laces broken. Loud yells were still coming from the Butt, and with a start, I realized that noisy hour was in progress.

Finally I got up and walked down the stairs to the Butt, kicking at a few skis on the way. I stood in the door of the Butt and looked at the screaming hordes of girls until Barbie saw me. Barbie had more sense about the expression on a human face than most people twice her age, which was twenty. She came to me instantly.

"How come I had to wait four days to find out what is going on around here?" I said furiously.

Barbie smiled her radiant smile, but her blue eyes were watchful. "We don't tell you everything, Mrs. M. If we did, you would go nuts."

I beckoned to her to come out into the corridor.

"Does the whole dorm know about this?"

"I guess so. She just goes around telling everyone as if it is everyday news. And the kids keep coming to me because I am going to be in medicine. They are so dumb that they ask me what happens if they quit taking the Pill—and I tell them that is when they are most fertile—they don't even know *that*."

Barbie was beautiful. With all her rainbow quality, she had a sense of humor barring her from sentimentality. Out near the basement stairs Virgie was talking to one of the freshmen in a loud voice about sex.

Barbie called out, "Hey, Virgie! Cool it," and put her finger to her lips. Then she turned back to me.

"Let's go upstairs," she said, and on the way she looked at me with the expression of an anxious aunt. We went into my sitting room and closed the door.

Barbie said, "I try to tell them what the facts are." She sat down and sprawled, looking troubled.

"What about those meetings on sex, and the doctor who was over here answering questions? It seemed to me they asked mostly about the cramps."

"Oh, well, Tuttle and I have figured out that about fifty

90

percent of them are still virgins, and the other fifty percent think they are too smart to get caught."

"How can you tell who is a virgin?"

"It's easy—by the way they talk and compare notes." She sighed. "No one can tell them that every time they have intercourse they are taking chances."

"On creating a new life, a *person*."

Barbie, who had respect for life, reverence for life, said, "Yes." She looked solemn.

"I wish the abortion laws were not so impossible! And what about the boy? Most of the time the boy isn't ready at all. This boy Becky loves is only a freshman in college." I was too involved, too caught in my memories of teen-age boys who got married. I had known what happened to some of them, the misery of poor jobs, the shouldering of what they were not adult enough to bear without bitterness.

"She won't hear of an abortion—don't think about that." Seeing that I had tears in my eyes, she came and put an arm around my shoulders and gave me a hug. "Don't take it so hard. Personally, I think Becky is lying."

"What on earth *for?*" I was startled.

"I don't know. But she's a born liar, and no one pays any attention to her."

"I can't help her unless she comes to me."

"That's *right*."

There was a knock on the door, and Phyllis stuck her head in. "Am I interrupting something?"

"Hi, Piss," Barbie said. Phyllis was not often on the scene, and I suspected she was one of the "sluts."

"Come on in," I said. Phyllis came in dressed in a short and transparent blue nightgown and sat down on the floor to do her calculus—very strange. I surmised she was frightened about the recent developments. Then Virgie came in and we all sat in a moody silence; for once, Virgie had nothing to say. We began grumbling about how we could not get to know the freshmen fast enough. I got up and left them and put a note under Becky's door saying not to feel alone and to come and talk if she wanted to. Then I went to bed and cried, worn out by the whole mess.

The next morning, I wanted some advice so I went over to the infirmary and asked Mrs. Bennett what to do. We sat in her office. Mrs. Bennett looked cool and competent in her white uniform and starched cap.

"You can only offer and then leave it up to her. We have quite a few pregnancies every year, Mrs. Martin. And we cannot take responsibility for that." She looked at me kindly through her spectacles.

I said, "We are caught. We have to let the girls be adults when they are not, and they are not because they have been kept as willful children for too long; if we try to advise them, they don't like it, and if we don't advise them, they don't like that, either."

"You are right, my dear. But weren't you that way once upon a time?"

I reflected. "Yes, but I was afraid to sleep with a boy."

"Well, they aren't. And this is the difference."

I told Mrs. Bennett about the rape scene.

"The poor kid," she said. "Maybe she thought that would give her a miscarriage." She got up and prepared to go; the interview was over. But on the way back to the dorm, I hugged my coat around me against a sharp wind and thought about what was bothering me. If a girl has passed out, how can she count how many boys raped her?

Two days passed, and I saw Becky only once, when I was walking over to the Administration Building to get her folder out of the dean's file in order too discover if there was anything in it to enlighten me. I met Becky coming back from class, and we stopped momentarily, standing in the wet, soggy leaves and fog, shivering. She looked pale and grey, but this was not unusual. She was not going to open the conversation.

"Did you get my note?" I said.

She merely nodded her head.

"Come and see me any time you feel like it." I felt sorry for her, yet in her face I could not see any emotion.

"O.K., thank you," she said, and walked on.

In her folder I saw that Becky's high school counselor had reported her as "responsible, and interested in ethics." How a

92

college is to judge a student by the recommendations that come in, I wouldn't know—all of them say lovely things.

That evening it was almost midnight when I pulled the white candlewick spread off my bed, got undressed, and climbed in with a copy of *Zelda*, feeling comfortable with three pillows, snug against the unrelenting fog and damp outside. Then there was a knock at the door. It was Becky, dressed in limp green and white sleeping culottes, with her knitting in her hands. I was too tired to stand on ceremony, so I did not budge.

"Can I talk to you?"

I put my book down on the pink blanket. "Yes, come in and sit in the armchair."

Becky sat down and tucked her feet cross-legged under her. She began knitting furiously and dropped a stitch; there was a silent interval while she picked it up. I pulled up the afghan, for my feet were cold, and dug my head into the pillows.

"What are you knitting?" I said. It was yards and yards of dark green.

"A sweater for Michael. I hope he likes it and I hope it fits." I was chilled by the colorless quality of her voice. Another silence.

Then without any preliminaries, she went on. "Well," she said, knitting busily, "I went to visit Michael's parents last weekend, and it was hard, but I didn't tell them anything. And I saw the doctor I've had ever since I was a little girl, and he has been giving me the Pill for four years to keep my periods regular."

I boggled a bit at this, thinking, this child has been on the Pill since she was fourteen. And why did she go to see Michael's parents instead of her own? She looked like a figurine, sitting there cross-legged, with a round face, short hair, and her eyes bent over her knitting.

"The doctor said he would give me the rabbit test, so he did, and I will know in a few days whether it is negative or positive—he said sometimes the first test is wrong."

Her tone was flat to the point of negation. I could not tell what she was hoping.

"I do wish you hadn't told all the girls about this," I said. "To them it is just a piece of gossip." My mind was a bit unhinged when I thought of the rape scene. How could Becky *know* four boys had raped her if she was unconscious? Who counted them? Who was there? Had she wanted to find violence, disgust? Or was she one of those unhappy people who can lose themselves only in sex, and the rest of the time wander about feeling alone?

There was no hint of this now. In the midnight silence, with the lamp casting a soft light over my bed, Becky sat knitting as efficiently as my mother had.

"I had to tell somebody, so I told Pat—she is the only one I can really talk to." But this was not the whole truth; she had told half a dozen girls at least.

Along my nerves I felt that Becky wanted to have a baby the way a little girl wants a big doll, that she would be disappointed, deprived of drama, blocked from leaving college and becoming domestic, if the test proved to be negative. But the baby wasn't real. It was a pawn in a sick game. The silence was prolonged.

"I wish you had told some responsible adult, because too much time has gone by—and what with the death in your family, even if you have told your mother, she has *too much* to deal with right now." I decided to plunge in as if the test would prove to be positive. "What are your feelings about abortion?"

She shook her head firmly and stopped knitting; the sharp needles were poised in the air. "I wouldn't have that, and I wouldn't give my baby for adoption. I would *have it*. I love Michael too much to do away with his baby."

"Michael is only a boy. Isn't he a freshman in college, too? You would have to be supported by his parents and yours. What would you do for a living?"

She by-passed this question. "He wants to be responsible, and he is so far away, and I am sorry. I wish I could see him. And when we talk to our parents, he should be with me. He's flunking out of college anyway. And I don't like school, I would rather be a housewife."

It seemed rather early in the year to be talking of flunking out of college. Nothing made any sense except that Becky intended to have her own way. She was a fake miniature of a woman; she wanted to reassure her man, but at the same time, she viewed him at this moment in terms of convenience. Or was I being unfair? Her lack of emotion froze me; she spoke as if she were talking about playing house in the world of childhood, where everything was provided.

"What about the baby? Having a baby means you will have to bring it up—the baby will be a real person. And you and Michael can never be young again; that is, you cannot be free to run around and make choices about your education, things like that." I could feel the poverty of spirit, the squalor, the resentment, all of which were part of Becky like a dull, grey tarnish that had nothing to do with a new life. "If he does marry you, ten years from now he may be angry."

She was knitting again, and I wished she would stop and look at me, but the needles clicked on as automatically as those of Madame de Farge. Now and then she looked up for an instant, but never long enough for our eyes to meet.

"Well, maybe I'm not going to have the baby." She was determined to evade any practical questions. "But if I do, I am going home and have it, and that is that."

I wondered if Becky's parents were going to pay a heavy price for always giving her what she wanted, or to the contrary, not giving her some emotional satisfaction she craved. I had a mental picture of them saying to their friends, "Well, here is Becky, and she is going to have a baby." It did not fit with the kind of girl she was, and they had two little boys of their own.

I felt inadequate. "What you need is a good social worker," I said despairingly. No response. I tried another tack.

"I have one idea for you. If you love Michael and he loves you, I think you should not go out with other boys until everything is settled."

This startled her. "I only go out with boys who are friends."

"The girls don't know that." I began to feel she was a tramp. Something was missing. She felt no guilt, no concern for anyone but herself; she was not prepared to change her ways for even a few weeks. And we were not prepared to take care of pregnant girls who advertised their predicament, more was the pity.

"The college wouldn't let you stay here, unless you were very dedicated and working hard," I said. "And then it would be only for a little while." This made no impression.

She changed the subject again, and caught me off guard. "I always dreamed about someone like you." This was devastating. What did she dream of? An older person who would level with her? I was so damn tired. I could imagine Becky having the baby and bringing it back to be admired—her only achievement, that of the female who has fulfilled her primitive function.

I did not want to talk about me. "If we were in the South Sea Islands, you might start sleeping with boys when you reached the age of puberty, and the older people would take care of you—you would live with them until you were ready to take care of yourself and your family. None of this old stuff about going to school. You can't make it here like that. You want your parents to give you money and leave you alone. It isn't fair." As I said this, I realized that I was old-fashioned and was getting nowhere.

"I wish I did live in the South Seas, then," flatly.

Something about the way we bring up our children, spoiling them until their bodies are adult while their emotions remain infantile, flooded me with nausea. I could imagine Becky and Michael blaming their parents for the rest of their lives and collecting emotional blackmail. If the parents were too protective, they would hate them for it, and if the parents tossed them out to make it on their own, they would whine and come home with the baby. I thought they would have more babies; but the hour was so late that I had lost my sense of perspective.

"Listen," I said, "I feel like sitting all the girls down and telling them that every time they have intercourse they are taking the responsibility for a new life, pills or not. Plenty of married people are still having babies they did not expect."

This got to her. She squirmed in the chair and stopped her interminable knitting for Michael. I hurt from the painful exercise we call "getting at the truth." It was so late, and my bedroom had lost its feeling of rest. From time to time someone would knock and be told to go away.

96

Finally Becky said, "I know it is dumb, but lots of kids in this dorm are sleeping with their boyfriends and I am the only one who got caught. That isn't a very high percentage."

"Don't talk to me about percentages. Every single one is the same old story, and the year is young." I was close to preaching. "You want adult pleasures without adult responsibilities."

She dodged again. "Well, maybe it was not true and the test will be negative again this time." (Could she be making all this up?) Then she bristled. "And if I am not going to have a baby, I hope my mother hasn't told my father. They would try to keep me from seeing Michael, and they can't do that."

What's the difference, I thought wearily. If it isn't Michael, it will be somebody else. Where was the dean's idea now? Keeping out of the girls' affairs, assuming they were old enough to learn the hard way? One night they would be playing with paper flowers or rolling on the floor like puppies, and the next we were talking about a baby who might be a fantasy, or who even now might be assuming a human shape in the body of this stubborn child. Nature was indomitable and none of us were any match for her.

As I lay there in silence, Becky got up and tucked her knitting under her arm. "You are so good to us it's fantastic," she said. *Fantastic* was the most overworked word in their vocabulary, unless it was *cool* or *groovy*. I didn't believe a word of this. Becky was a great con artist.

The next day Pat came in, still looking elegant and something else—relieved but cross. "Did you talk to Becky?

"Yes. I got nowhere at all."

"Have you heard the latest? She called up her doctor at home and he said the test was negative. Isn't that something?"

"It is indeed." What was really wrong with Becky was not settled.

"The funny thing is that I think Becky is disappointed." Pat tossed her long pony tail and looked bewildered.

No wonder. There were still the four boys who had raped Becky; I felt like hanging a sign on her that said, "This girl is dangerous." Becky could still have a baby and it wouldn't be Michael's.

One evening we looked at "A Man and a Woman" on TV, drawn together to escape the damp cold weather, which seemed to penetrate into our very souls. Pat, who was nearsighted, sat near the TV with her feet up on a chair, participating by crying, cussing the "bad guys," cooing over romance, and delivering mini-lectures; Pat was the old-fashioned girl, who exists in our society even yet.

Becky sat with her back against the love seat where I was more or less reclining, my feet propped on one of the arms; she was knitting as usual.

"How's the sweater coming along?" I asked.

"Very well." She held it up and it was enormous. It reminded me of the greeting card lady who began knitting a scarf and ended with a volley ball net.

Becky's tone was imperturbable. I kept wishing she would move away from me a few inches, and it bothered me that I could not be more objective. The back of a human head is dear and vulnerable, or it is not. Becky had acquired a phony aura of the experienced woman; everyone was polite to her, but she was no longer part of the group. She had a condescending air.

It was a cold, mean night some weeks later when the very air was frozen and lay motionless against the windowpanes, when the snow lay outside in rough sculptured blocks thrown like immense teeth from the snow plows, and the street lamps shone down on a landscape as sterile as moon dust, that I finally came to know Becky.

She came into my room, drab and expressionless, with her cropped hair jagged along the back of her neck, and her face, pock-marked and as colorless as her voice, dressed in a wilting robe of brown and white cotton, a robe like a potholder, worn and washed and serviceable. I wondered if Becky's mother was responsible for never buying her anything gay, colorful, or

98

foolish. I could not feel in her the living tremor, the fresh scent of youth, but felt rather an old, decaying fear.

She was wearing a small diamond ring, the stone small as a crumb of glass, on her left hand. She sat for awhile looking at the TV.

We did not talk. I wondered later whether if I had tried harder to draw her out, what happened might have been avoided, but this was useless speculation. Much later, I went to bed.

It was almost one in the morning when I was drowsing, with the vaporizer and the warm electric blanket shutting away the marble zero of the world outside, that the knocking started on my bedroom door. There were four girls outside. Becky and her roommate, Ginevra, were hysterical.

Becky said wildly, with more emotion that I had ever seen in her, "We have had two dresses solen from our closets, our best dresses, one from my closet and one from Gin's."

"I'm sick of this," Ginevra said. She was dark and slim, radiant with life, her long hair shining, all softness and silk and color, physically gentle.

"We want to look in everyone's closet," Becky said.

"All right," I said. "But who would hang them in a closet?"

The nightmare began. Upstairs there were rustlings and cries. "Come on," I said to Willie. "Let's look in the suitcases in the luggage room."

The luggage room was a tomb in the basement, next to the old boiler that roared day and night. We picked our way carefully, opening and closing every suitcase. All of them were empty. The emptiness of all departures seemed to fill me and take away my heart. Here in the night, we were moving in slow motion through a bad dream.

By the time we got back upstairs, the whole first floor was trembling in a nervous silence. Where was Barbie?

"She has an overnight," Willie said. I went in my sitting room and sat down to think, but almost immediately Beatrice, who was in charge during Barbie's absence, came to me. Her large brown eyes were wide with worry.

"One of the girls says you must look in Becky's and

Ginevra's room. It isn't fair to look everywhere else and leave them out."

"All right." I called the campus police and two of them came, a big burly man who would have made a good Santa Claus, and a little pudgy man named Homer.

"We will stay while you search the room," the big one said. "We can't go in without a search warrant. Go in by yourself and take the girl who is in charge and put everyone else out."

I went to get Beatrice, and the campus police settled themselves in two chairs in the living room. The sight of them made Becky frantic. Her movements were jerky; her eyes dilated.

"Do you have any objection to our searching *your* room? I said to Becky and Gin. Becky objected, but Gin said, "Go ahead."

"I can't clear everything until we do this," I said to Becky. "After all, we can't go through everyone else's room, as you have, and leave you out. It wouldn't be fair."

So Beatrice and I went in and shut the door. It was then that I began to have a crawling sickness in my stomach. I had never before searched through the private possessions of anyone, except after a death in the family. Beatrice began on Ginevra's dresser, and I took Becky's. We worked in silence with hushed sighs and squeamish comments.

"Becky is a very neat person," I said. In each drawer, I found tidy little piles of humble belongings, panties, bras, pajamas, all of them clean and folded. The top of the dresser was bare. There were none of the ribbons, the mementoes, the pictures that most girls stuff away or scatter under their mirrors. There was an arid feeling, and I grew emptier as I lifted up the little piles and tried not to disturb them.

Beatrice was in the closet when I finished, bringing down boxes from the shelf. The closet was dark and very few clothes hung in it. "There's a locked suitcase in here," she said in a muffled voice.

When we got the suitcase out, we called to Becky and Ginevra. "If you will open this suitcase, we will be finished, thank heaven."

100

Becky had turned pasty. "I don't know where the keys are—I have lost them." I lifted the suitcase; it was so heavy that I could not carry it. By now it was two in the morning, and I was exhausted.

We stood in the middle of the room. On Ginevra's side, there were posters of scrawly designs in deep magenta, purple, green, and red, tinged with the fantasies of imagination, viscera in a dream. There was a travesty on the old drugstore Indian who at one time indicated a cigar shop; he had a hat on an and was smoking grass according to the caption, *Cannabis Rex*. But this side of the room looked lived in. Ginevra was an art major and had a penchant for burning incense and working by an old lamp with a Tiffany glass shade; she lived as if aware of her fantasies, much as we lived in our youth among a collection of "Memory Books," full of dance programs and dead corsages, and with pennants on the walls.

On Becky's side of the room, so little existed that I wondered if she had already moved out as she was planning to do after exams. But I recalled, with a shock, that she had sent home a large trunk, and before that, I had seen a pile of stuffed animals ready to be packed—those ubiquitous stuffed animals the girls collected as if they were unwilling to leave childhood, but were trying to do so with humor. Becky's side of the room looked the way a hotel room looks when the luggage is ready, and the phone is lifted to call the porter so one can check out.

The girls were nervous in the silence. Becky had become extremely agitated, and kept peeping out in the hall to look at the two ruddy policemen who sat resting their feet, like two old uncles waiting for dinner. As fearsome representatives of the Law, they would not have qualified.

"Just wait here, and I will ask what we should do," I said, and I went out, got the policemen and we went into my sitting room while the girls waited.

The big one said, "Get her permission to open the suitcase. After all, you have to, even if she is innocent." They peered at me with brotherly concern, and for a brief moment, I longed for them to take charge. Then they went out, but Homer turned and said, "We will be back on our rounds."

A strange suspension of time came over me, as if time had ceased its normal progression and was moving with unutterable slowness. I called Beatrice. "Tell Becky to come in here and I'll talk with her alone." I was almost too tired to think. My mind had turned to gelatin. It was a night when someone else beset by my particular set of hang-ups might have moved with more dispatch. I had, in the past, moved with the speed of lightning when a boy ran his arm through a glass door in my classroom and severed an artery—but to see anyone rendered helpless by shame turned me to jelly. Before me floated the memories of every cookie jar I had ever raided, every lie I had ever told, and then running to my mother to confess, for she never punished us if we told the truth. The sitting room, which had seemed so warm, so safe, was now the police station, cold, forbidding, impersonal.

Beatrice came back, looking frightened but determined, her eyes larger than ever. "Becky is pretending to be asleep; I called her three times and she did not answer."

"Well, let her sleep. But get the suitcase and bring it in here and we will see about it tomorrow." I felt a surge of pity for Becky, lying there alone and terrified. I could remember huddling under the covers and waiting for my father's temper tantrum, or worse, a long lecture.

But when Beatrice brought the suitcase, Becky came along and said, "I might be able to open it with a nail file. My father can, sometimes."

"You go to bed," I said to Beatrice, "and you stay here," to Becky, for at last I understood. Becky wanted to be caught.

When we were alone, I said to Becky, "If you put the dress in the suitcase, you locked it in there tonight, so you know where the keys are. And your dress that was stolen does not exist. Now I have to open the suitcase so I can say you did not take Ginevra's dress, if you did not. So tell me, did you take the dress?" I was trying to speak very gently, for the words were harsh.

"Yes," she said, and covered her face with her hands. "I feel terrible." But she did not cry.

"Then will you get me the keys? And we will take it out.

Then you can take your suitcase back to your room. Tomorrow I will give Ginevra's dress back to her, and I shall not tell anyone where I found it. You and I can work this out together."

"I don't know where the keys are. And you haven't found out where *my* dress is." She was still lying. From what twisted corner of her brain did her reasoning come?

"All right. May *I* open the suitcase?"

"Yes." Her face was a mask. "But may I go now?"

It was very simple. She did not want to be there when I opened it.

"All right. Go back to bed and I will do it later."

Beatrice was still in the hall; she had shared too much to be sent away now. We both went and got our luggage keys. I was still bewildered by Becky, but I understood that she was not able to face the evidence directly. I got one of the locks open, but the other resisted obstinately. We worked in silence.

Then I went to my box full of odds and ends, things that were borrowed so often, and got a small screwdriver.

We pried open the stubborn lock, and there lay Ginevra's silk dress like a rainbow on top of a pile of packed records, books, sexy underwear, scarves, and other little things - blue silk garters, ribbons of many colors.

Beatrice stood in shock. "I don't believe it." But she went off to bed. I got up. It was three in the morning and my legs were giving way. Out in the hall, I found Becky had returned and was waiting.

"I'll talk to you tomorrow," I said. All warmth and trust were gone, and I was cold to my bones.

Later on, I couldn't do much of anything. The dean tried, then called Becky's parents, and Becky called up a boy who came and took her away skiing for two days.

Ginevra came in and said the little diamond ring was hers, and that Becky firmly denied it, so she had let her go on wearing it.

"You must make her give it back." It took the dean to make Becky admit the ring belonged to Ginevra, and finally, one evening in this long and terrible week, Gin made her give it back after they talked for three long hours. Becky insisted it was her engagement ring, and she loved Michael too much to take it off. (Shades of the false pregnancy!)

"She cried and cried," Ginevra said. But with everyone else, Becky maintained her dreary cool, as if nothing at all had happened. In the suitcase we found fancy panties, a bikini pair with ruffles of bright pink, and a green pair with wide lace; these belonged to Gin also.

"I always wanted to be friends with you, and I never made it," Becky cried to Ginevra. "So I wanted to hurt you."

Is this the story one might call "The Thief"? For it was not economic need that made Becky steal; she stole only things that mean love. We found records that belonged to various people, and two volumes of Rod McKuen inscribed to Becky from her brothers in her own handwriting. We found a hand-crocheted dress and a green sweater belonging to Becky's "best friend" in Oliver dorm, and the friend came over, bringing paper bags of records she said Becky had brought to her saying, "Because someone has been stealing from me, and I want you to keep these safe." We never found a fur coat belonging to Jane across the hall, and I wondered if it had been shipped off in the trunk.

We all felt rather sick. For days, we moved in a chill atmosphere. Becky's parents said they would get psychiatric treatment for her. Becky went home. Ginevra, during the few days they had together, showed compassion, but Ginevra's mother was hysterical, phoning me every day to find out what we were doing.

Barbie said it all. "It isn't losing our things, it is losing Becky. It is not trusting any more." Barbie kept her sorrow to herself; Beatrice cried big tears. Both girls were true to their natures.

"I guess the freshmen are a new generation," Barbie said. I wondered if they were, but I didn't tell Barbie what I thought. She seemed older, and had lost one of her illusions.

After Becky went home, her parents found Jane's fur coat in the trunk and sent it back to us.

Warm Embers

There was not much time for brooding in Bixby dorm. My encounters with the girls were nearly always brief. Everything came my way as fast as one box after another on an assembly line, and I was too busy catching the next box to feel its weight. In the case of Becky, I took several days to recover, but life soon took on its normal pattern. I found increasingly that life was full of surprises, something I cannot say about the practices of my own generation—we nearly always do what is expected, following familiar patterns that tend to become ruts.

One day after lunch I went to the staircase and bawled for Barbie; my voice, which was usually soft, had taken on a strange new tendency to yell, and I rather enjoyed this. Yelling was liberating. Barbie came down, bouncing as ever, and we went to the sitting room to talk.

"This morning three girls were sleeping in the living room. They had all the cushions off the couches and they were sleeping on these lined up in front of the fireplace. They were wrapped in blankets like mummies with only their hair sticking out, so I don't know who they were. Are you going to let them do this?"

Barbie beamed her sunflower smile. "Well, it's fun. I remember we used to do it last year. Did they wake you up last night?"

"No, I didn't hear a sound. I suppose they went to sleep looking at the fire, but what if it gets to be a mass movement? Can't you imagine the living room floor covered with sleeping mummies?"

At this she laughed outright. "I suppose this would be like exam week. Wait till you see *that*. Only then they are all sitting up." She grew thoughtful. "I would let them do it only on Saturday night. Mrs. Perley doesn't come on Sundays, and hardly anyone gets up in the morning."

I tried temporizing. "When I was first married, my husband and I once took all the mattresses in the house and piled them one on top of the other, then we climbed up on top of the heap and just lay there and laughed."

Barbie blushed a pale wild rose pink, but she laughed also. Her eyes had turned a deeper blue. She wasn't going to answer that one.

"O.K.," I said. "But make them wait until well after Saturday midnight when the boys are out of the dorm—and sometimes boys come in early Sunday morning for ski dates in winter, or days outdoors in fine weather."

"They don't mind the boys." (An understatement if ever I heard one!)

"Well, until the rules are changed. . . ." I didn't know what to say. One thing I had not become accustomed to was seeing girls running around downstairs in short nightgowns with their hair in rollers when dates were coming in, but I knew I couldn't do anything about it.

Barbie gave in, although I sensed that she thought I was a bit behind the times. She was playing with a ball point pen—click, click.

"I'll make them ask permission every time," she said, "and there won't be too many of them."

She went upstairs to her books and I tried to remember what is so great about sleeping on the floor. Could it have been that being cramped up in a little room gets tiresome. Oh, those roommate discontents! And was it fun to feel the expanse of a big room, with the firelight playing, the shadows in corners, and conversations murmuring? I supposed so. I remembered the slumber parties of my youth, when my father left the house entirely, and twenty girls took over the whole house and stayed awake all night talking and giggling. On one occasion at least, I wanted to go to sleep at breakfast time, and my mother said, "No, you don't. You will stay up until everyone is fed."

I feared that my irritation over this new project came from the old parental feeling of wanting everyone in her own room and asleep, at least after two in the morning. With a shiver, I realized that it would be three o'clock and later, all night if the Student Government got its way. Silence! It was the thing I missed most. Saturday night was bad enough without having them end up outside my door!

Ellen Writes Her Story

One evening Ellen came in with a paragraph of a short story, and sat down on the floor in the middle of my bedroom, looking serious. I had not seen her for weeks, except to say, "Hi," as I seemed to be saying over forty-nine times a day. Now I looked at her and remembered my first impression: beautiful in a dark, smouldering way, tall, with clothes that said money— or was it the way Ellen wore them? She was dressed in a blue sweatshirt with a white turtleneck under it, nothing extraordinary about that.

"Remember Parent's Weekend?" she said. Yes, I did. Who could forget it? Ellen's father, Mr. Zabriskie, was a rotund lawyer in his sixties, who was vulnerable to a woman yet uneasy in her presence. Ellen's brother, a tall, good-looking boy from M.I.T., had come also. Ellen said afterwards, "He's everything a girl could want in a big brother." What a prolonged Open House that weekend was! I had no time to be more than polite.

"I'm trying to write my story for Mr. Taylor."

"For heaven's sake. I thought that was due a long time ago."

"Yes, but he gave me an extension because I find it so hard

to do. I'm trying to write about the time my mother left." Her eyes were vaguely moist.

"When was that?"

"When I was twelve." Silence. "It's funny, but I can't remember when she left at all. I just remember my father sitting on one of their twin beds and telling me she was gone." Her voice was quiet, as if she was digging up something hard to face.

"Maybe you blocked it out. We can do that when something to too painful to bear. Or maybe you weren't there when she left."

"She tried to commit suicide twice—she has a long scar on her arm."

"When did you see her after she left?"

"Oh, not for about two years."

"When did you see her last?"

"Two years ago."

I was stunned. "Where does she live?"

"In Georgia—she married again."

"Well, you can use the memories of the past, several years apart, and some flashbacks when you were little—and what you thought about in between."

She got up, and so did I. When they decided to go, I had to let go very fast, but it was still difficult for me. It was like letting go of a young swimmer in the middle of a strong current pulling her out to sea. We walked out to the stairs. She climbed a few steps, and at a safe distance from me, she turned and stood, elegant and tired. I made one more try.

"It's hard for anyone to write—someone said it takes as much out of you as a stiff game of tennis. Maybe you should take something else, a less poignant experience."

She shook her head. "No. This is the most traumatic thing that ever happened to me, and I am going to write it."

She had discovered the secret. When she got it on paper, it would be out of herself; she was going to create some order from her personal chaos. She ran up the stairs.

The next evening Ellen's pain was back. I was reading Hortense Calisher's *The New Yorkers*, when Ellen knocked at the door and came in. Navy blue and pink. She was a complex girl who could relax and be a "real slob" if she felt like it, but she never lost her casual flair. Now she looked a bit disheveled.

"I am having an awful time—I guess I feel very insecure." She held out a page of handwriting. "This little bit took me two hours. Would you read it?"

I could scarcely resist the imploring look, but I said, "I don't think it is a good idea for me to read what you are doing until you finish—I might say the wrong thing."

But she was looking for her mother in more ways than one. She hesitated, then handed her paper over to me, whether I would or no. The writing was pale in tone compared to what she had told me, with her large eyes almost brimming over. Now she had begun her story with a young girl who was quite calm and objective.

"I think you must get your reader sympathizing right from the start—this kid sounds as if she is covering up how she feels and getting away with it."

"That's what I always do." Yes. This was how she had borne with her father who, it was rumored, had been married five times. I looked hard at Ellen, and decided she was really in trouble. She was sitting in a chair with her feet twisted around each other at the ankles.

"Why not begin with loneliness, the vacuum inside where everything feels grey, and even the most beautiful house, the loveliest day, is gloomy? Begin with the awful sense of loss."

She grabbed her paper and went out. This time I hoped I had not suggested the impossible. A week or so later, Ellen brought me her completed story, beautifully typed and enclosed in clear plastic. "Tomorrow I have to go to court to testify for my father's divorce." I opened the paper with a feeling of gooseflesh along my arms—the feeling we get when a human being struggles to create something true. It was all there, Ellen's patience to render something faithfully, no matter what it cost her.

Yet, as I read, with her eyes on me, looking for some small expression on my face, I found myself stopping to say, "You haven't put in the bitterness."

"I don't want it to be bitter. I want it to be just the same old

110

thing, over and over, and how a girl of twelve or thirteen can know what is going on." She got down on the floor, rolled over on her stomach and put her hands under her chin.

"Have you got a title?"

She sat up, shook her head, and smiled. The Mona Lisa? Enigmatic, but too fat. Merle Oberon? Closer. And before I could say anything else, she got up and took the paper.

"It is very much better," I said. "Good going."

I was so sure we had finished with Ellen's story that I was not prepared when she came in one night with a new version. I really thought we had done it, for another week had elapsed. This time the story looked much longer. I was reading the newspaper, and Ellen sat down on the floor, then lay down on her stomach as before and said, "Can I do my corrections here?"

"You certainly may," I said, and went back to rustling the paper which had all sorts of dismal news on student revolts and the war in Vietnam. Ellen turned pages slowly.

Finally she looked up. "I spent all week on this. Will you read it? Her tone had changed; now she spoke with the voice of someone who is proud of something she wants to share.

I took the manuscript, secretly impressed with her discontent, her willingness to abandon the beautiful copy with the plastic cover. Before my eyes there now unfolded the work of the writer in revision; it was as if I had seen a foggy snapshot where no details were discernible; now the concrete details leaped to life: the heavy mahogany of the divorce court where a young girl saw it all as an athletic contest for prizes and the judge as a referee, where she saw the house remodeled for each new wife, and the sop to the child's pride in her redecorated bedroom of white and gold and turquoise, the acres of white carpets, the beautiful house bombed in a horrible scene when the last wife screamed, "Your mother was a Lesbian, did you know that, Ellen? Your mother was a Lesbian!" A new word striking the child again and again with the lie to destroy her, to have revenge, and Ellen and her father running into the bathroom to lock themselves in and cry in each other's arms.

I could hardly speak. I was limp with what children have to endure and what they survive. Ellen lay now flat on her back.

When she heard the pages had stopped turning and were lying silently in my hands, she looked up.

"The awful thing is that it's all true, and I still haven't got a title."

"Well, you have got it out of yourself and on to paper, so it can never hurt quite so much again. How about a title suggesting something that goes in circles round and round, and the girl knows it, but she can't stop it? Damn it all," I said. "These are adult children who expected you to be grown up."

In the face of Ellen's tough sadness and courage, a painful moment surfaced, one of those moments of truth burned into the psyche for good. It was of my own little girl coming into the master bedroom where one twin bed was empty and neatly made up, and saying, "Where is my Daddy?" What was happening to me? Everything that happened to the girls was forcing me to remember all the buried-and-done-with parts of myself.

"I am divorced, Ellen," I said.

She meditated, then shook her head. She rolled over and propped up her head with one hand. "It wasn't like this, I'll bet."

"No, it wasn't like this."

"Mr. Taylor gave me lots of extra time. He's cool. He says maybe the father is in love with his daughter. It was rough when he asked me to read it in class, but I did it."

I tried to feel quiet. "Well, maybe Mr. Taylor is right about the father. If the daughter is the only woman who has been faithful, who is always *there*—but she has outgrown all that, and the father hasn't. Santayana says, 'He who does not remember his own past is condemned to live it over again.' The father is living it over and over. It's like a spiral."

Ellen thought. "I wonder if he will marry *again*." Her eyes held the fear that she would always have to take care of him. "He is sixty-five and I am only nineteen."

The room had grown curiously abstract, like a shadowy background in a painting where one apprehends only a single figure in the foreground. Ellen, with her sophisticated facade, her money, became someone else—Antigone? Having only her loyalty, her human fear that it might be up to her, that she might have to give up her own life.

112

"You will find your own man and have your own home," I said firmly. "And your brother will have his home, and the younger men will help you—your husband and your brother—you will manage among you."

She seemed far away, yet very close, lying on my old oriental rug. I realized with a start that I had not even heard the noises in the hall. Was Ellen still working on the shocking statement about her mother? The Greeks had a word for everything—Lesbos, the Island of Sappho, had become in our time a word for perversion; the word itself had become perverted, meaning too many different things.

"Listen, Ellen," I said, plunging, "your mother tried to commit suicide twice—you told me about the scars on her arms. Are you going to believe lies about her without ever asking? She has married again. Why couldn't it be that under more stress than she could bear, she couldn't manage and went away because she was not well enough to be a good mother to you?"

She looked better; the rose color was coming up in her cheeks. Privately I was damning the vicious stepmother who could take out her fury on a child. If there were any married Lesbians hanging out in this domestic morass, my vote would have gone to the stepmother, a real old fairy-tale character indeed.

Ellen did not answer. Then she said at last, smiling, her face back in focus, "Maybe I will think of a title in the middle of the night."

"You might very well do that. How about 'The Family Album,' since you have organized it around looking at old snapshots?"

She shook her head. She was safe from letting me give her any suggestions on a name for her brain child. Getting up as swiftly and awkwardly as a young deer, she ran out, and I could hear her yelling in the hall, "Hey Virgie! How about going down to the Busy Bee and getting some chocolate doughnuts?"

The calliope voice of Virgie floated down from the third floor, and the front door slammed soon afterwards.

Ellen's father's latest divorce was finally settled after a sordid court battle. I came in one night out of the incessant rain that turned to unnerving sheets of ice, and said to Ellen, "I am really tired of this awful weather." She was sitting in the living room typing away at the homework she had left for four days to go home and take care of her father. Her hair was pushed behind her ears and she wore no make-up. She looked self-possessed.

Struggling with my boots, I asked, "Well, how did it all come out?"

She made a moue of disgust. "Dad had some dirty stuff on her, like an affair with another man. But she wants $85,000 and the house. I didn't sleep and I was sick at my stomach—I kept throwing up—and I slept on the couch in Dad's apartment." In spite of all this, she did not sound cross.

"All she wants is money, really. My Dad's lawyer offered her $5,000 and then $35,000."

"I hope he gets the divorce for your sake," I said, sitting down for a bit on the living room floor.

She smiled at me as if I were not very adult.

"I hope he gets it for *his* sake." Not once, I thought, going to my room, had she ever expressed anything but love for her father or her mother.

Ellen came in a few days later and said her father got his divorce, but he had to pay $17,000 and lawyer's fees. She still felt sorry for him. "That woman really took us for a ride," she said crossly. "I asked him if he would like to sell my car, but he said no."

I was going to be haunted by this story, every time I saw Ellen taking girls in her car, opening her billfold to pay, losing her cigarettes and records, going out on dates.

Her eyes turned warm, as if reassuring the old was her natural instinct. "Hey, I'm *trying* to find my own man."

I couldn't help smiling. "Give yourself plenty of time."

"My father can't do a thing for himself. I guess he fell in love with women who took care of him and then they didn't do it any more. They just wanted what his money could buy."

"Well, dear girl, you have it all pegged in the story—the closets overflowing with expensive clothes, the cars, the decorators. *Bravo*. How you got to be so honest, I can't imagine."

Now she grinned. "It's my form of rebellion," she said, and went out.

It was after midnight when Ellen left me that night, and the house was quiet. I remembered the story said that her grandma was the only one who was ever a real mother to her. I wondered if some day I would see a novel by Ellen Zabriskie.

Why Am I Here?

In my studio across the way, I continued to spend my mornings recording my thoughts in my journal. Ellen's last remark, "It's my form of rebellion," reverberated for some days. Continuously through the year I recalled the day I decided to come here. Coming here was my form of rebellion, my refusal to accept declining into uselessness.

November, January, and March are months I could easily do without in New England, and this November had been so intense that I scarcely noticed, beyond a brief irritation now and then, the mugginess of the weather. Yet the mystery remained; I felt well. I felt needed. But being needed can be a great many different things; this seemed to me to be the trap. One can be needed by neurotics who have a "bottomless pit" no one can fill, or needed for what one does not want to do, or does badly.

What did Becky dream of? And what did Ellen dream of? Whatever Becky was, she was a dreamer so far gone that dreaming turned into lies. And Ellen wanted to rebel by being honest.

My mind these days returned freely to the past, where the

116

days of my girlhood, then the college days, the teaching days, the time of being in love, were all coming together. I lived in an old house breathing fresh air, with girls running in and out, the creaking wood of the old structure holding screams and running feet, hands on the banisters, parties and studying and boys.

What I had not known last summer was the difference between teaching in a classroom by day and *living* with adolescents who were night owls. What I had long suspected, that the "generation gap" was more emotional than ideological, seemed to be proving itself. And as for the "gender gap" we are hearing so much about now, it strikes me as emotional also; are we casting off the traditional sex roles for reasons of equality? Or do we secretly long to be closer together? Or both?

In any case, I wanted, like Ellen, to be more honest. I had begun to see the girls as objects of Nature, females driven by opposing forces, the desire to get an education, and the even more powerful urge to mate and have children. In the fiery interlude of autumn, the final burst of warmth, when the cottony clouds hung motionless in a burning blue sky, the girls rolled in the fallen leaves, screaming with all the zest of children—with the coming of snow, they climbed into it, slid on it, fell into drifts, made "angels" by lying on their backs and waving their arms. I knew in the teaching days that any change in the weather would produce a restless rebellion against books and tight little desks and the everlasting voice of the teacher! But I had considered this something to be subdued if the work was to go on.

Oh well, I thought, now it is different. College is a last fling at childhood except in the classroom, a place of the first freedom away from home, where they can be sloppy or neat, swear or be prim, eat fast or slowly, dress like bums or ladies. College could discover lying or honesty, manners or rudeness, promiscuity or faithfulness. Not that I devalued the purpose of college, to develop the mind, but the mind could not be separated from the body, the heart; and I looked at a William Blake engraving I had enjoyed for years, "The Reunion of the Body and the Soul."

I was needed for what I had to give; it sounded banal, but

117

being here had brought me the immense satisfaction of giving myself the way I really was, not the way someone else wanted or imagined me to be. This rather simple thought made me euphoric. The old molds were broken, the mother, the teacher, the wife, the daughter, the sister, the grandmother—for all of these there had been expectations established by ancient customs, and breaking them brought pain. Was I discovering the fun of getting old? To be myself, to find it had become too late to be any of the things expected, to get it all together now; society no longer had anything to ask of me—and all the debts to *that* had been paid, with interest. What had I feared? Ailments, a long dying, poverty, all useless to fear, so unpredictable.

In my studio, I looked up at the high basement windows where snow was piling up to enclose this private space, and a bright geranium stood in a pot. This was a year to remember, it couldn't last always, but then, what could? The present had never seemed more exciting than now. I looked at a Matisse print on the wall, and the sunlight passing over its purple, green, rose. Now there was more of being than of doing; now there was, paradoxically, more time. I had forgotten calendars and days with bars on them. The carillon chimed from the clock tower, a gentle sound so familiar that I seldom heard it.

Monotony was always a way of life I found unbearable. To know what the next day would bring forth, with carefully chiseled plans to prevent untoward happenings, was never my style! The automatic could be done automatically; the unexpected had brought me the truths I found by myself.

It was almost time for Thanksgiving vacation, and I was glad of it. It was going to snow. At four, the sky was charcoal grey between the high panes of windows; the shadows were grey in the folds of white curtains. Far to the west, I could see a strange pink light behind the black trees, and overhead, the thick dark hung silently.

118

An Early Christmas

Somewhere back in the middle of my life, I decided that Christmas had become nothing but bills and chores and fatigue! And every year Christmas began to take over weeks, then months, before it happened, as I shopped, wrapped and mailed packages, fussed and fumed. Christmas. New Year's. The impossible and fearsome dragons we have created, monsters with golden scales and diamond eyes; Christmas and the Mardi Gras have become confused. Why must we hunt in shops for a gift to add to the incredible collection of objects belonging to Aunt Laura? Or listen, in a sleet that whips cruelly, to "Joy to the World" shuddering artificially from a supermarket, brayed through trumpets of synthetic angels? The whole world at Christmas seems to be stuffing its stomach, ears, and eyes, yet paradoxically still starving.

"I don't know what to get for Sarah, that old harridan—she has everything but a fur-lined bathtub," says a lady in chinchilla.

Whatever else women are doing at Christmas, they have to do the shopping, write notes to rectify their "neglect" of distant relatives; the imposition of the ideal, "'Tis the season to be

119

jolly," can turn into hysteria quietly contained. One longs to do a complete "cop-out," sit by the fire at home snug against the cold and dark and slush, but not alone. One longs to have the true feelings exposed, to enjoy the myth, to light candles, to go to sleep in the "close and holy darkness."

Was it only the year before I went to Wadleigh that I had reflected moodily on how it was no wonder Christmas produces a high suicide rate?

Rural New England has a great feeling for holidays; on the Fourth of July it has small-town parades, with fragmented bands tooting down the main streets, and flags hung out over white houses and green lawns. The Hallowe'en pumpkins burn like great orange owls in the windows of October, and stuffed scarecrows lean on front porches or stand tipsily in the brown fields. Holidays in America were born right here and they were all coming back to me with some old, ancestral memory that seemed to be in my bones.

So Christmas. In the dorm we burned up with a fine extravagance all the wood in our basement, nice dry wood that had been resting against the boiler. We put red candles on our living room mantel and lit up the sconces in the hall with tiny white ones. One evening, the maintenance men came in with a Christmas tree they had cut in the forest; it reached to our twelve-foot ceiling without dwarfing the room in the least. Barbie ran down to the basement, followed by a covey of girls, to find the Christmas lights and ornaments saved from previous years.

Some of the lights did not work—do they ever? So I went out to buy some new ones; when I returned late in the evening, my tires crunching over the snow, I saw dozens of faces pressed to the frosty window panes. Everyone who wasn't out on a date helped to decorate the Christmas tree.

Rae sat down on the floor and forgot about the problems of the world. She hunched her bare feet up under her nightgown and said, "I am going to sit up and look at it all night, and when I have children, this is how it is going to be."

When we were finished with the tree, Barbie sat down and read aloud that old chestnut, "The Littlest Angel," to an au-

120

dience stretched on the floor or sitting cross-legged in rapt attention. "Unless ye become as a little child, ye shall not enter the kingdom of heaven." This mood was all of a piece with Barbie shouting the Stevenson verse "How would you like to go up in the swing/ Up in the air so blue," whenever she felt especially good. Sophistication got short shrift around the dorm.

We all drew names for "Peter and Paul." Everyone was a Peter who had a Paul, and Peter would give Paul a tiny present every day for a week and a big present the last night before vacation. Getting up in the morning became getting up to one long Christmas day, with the snowy world outside spreading around us like a great frozen ocean of waves and foam, and the dorm inside sprinkled with little presents covered with bright paper, hidden in unlikely places or dangling from chandeliers. Notes were taped to doorjambs and banisters saying where to look. The presents were bubble gum, suckers, posters, mobiles made by hand, and hundreds of things people just decided to give away. One beautiful mobile was made of little walnut shell boats with tiny paper sails that quivered in the slightest breath of air.

My Peter gave me a leather Peace symbol to hang around my neck, and I wore it. The card said it was "to go with your bell-bottomed flannel slacks." My bell-bottomed slacks, it would seem, had inadvertently provided me with a ticket of admission. I realized that my custom of dressing like a proper lady in the afternoons had not fooled them a bit; now with the Peace symbol about my neck, I had accidentally joined the protest movement.

But my Peter went further the next day. Returning after dinner, I found the whole door of my bedroom covered with an immense poster of Sophia Loren, her admirable bosoms photographed under a soaking wet blouse. Relenting after this, my Peter gave me a tiny Santa Claus sock full of stick candy.

In the midst of this excitement, I presumed classes were still going on, for I heard the feet on the stairs going to classes, and the groans—"I have so much *work* to do!"

121

On the Sunday before vacation, we had our annual Christmas party for the faculty. The great flakes outside had formed tall drifts, and we could hear the snow shovels scraping on the walks—it stormed so hard that the guests were blown in the doors on gusts of wind, and stamped their boots, wheezing and puffing. My bed was loaded with wet coats. The girls came downstairs dressed up in velvet or silk, bright wools, with very short or very long skirts, their hair brushed until it shone, and sang carols sweetly; but later in the dining room, "Hark the Herald Angels Sing," was transmuted to, "Hark the Herald Angels Shout/Three More Days Till We Get Out!"

It was the night before vacation when we reached the grand climax of hysteria with the annual "Hootnanny" in the auditorium over in the arts center. I gazed unbelievingly at girls dressed in leather jackets and tight pants, with moustaches painted on their faces. Others were mysterious-looking whores, with long, low-necked dresses and masses of garish make-up. I had forgotten what girls look like with rouge and heavy dark lipstick. The noise and the screaming split my ears. If ever the girls had any inhibitions, these were forgotten in this mad Mardi Gras. Some girls had pillows stuffed over their stomachs and waddled around looking pregnant. Hadn't I read somewhere about a woman who could not stop eating, and during her wild stuffing, wore a pillow over her belly?

But all this may have spared us the explosions that come before any school holiday. For afterwards, we went back to the dorm for our own private party, and the crazy costumes were put away. We settled down by our Christmas tree to open our last "special presents," and the floor was covered with girls and seas of brightly colored paper; the air was full of delight, and the fire burned in the fireplace.

My Peter turned out to be Virgie, who gave me a white pottery candlestick with a red candle in it. And the bellowing Virgie came over to me like a shy little girl for a thank-you hug. My Paul was Willie, for whom I had bought a white woolly lamb. "His name is Martin," she said, "and I am going to take him home with me for vacation."

The dorm gave me a beautiful leather album with

snapshots of themselves in it, and I gave the dorm a four-slice toaster. When Barbie opened this, they gave me a "big fifteen" and yelled, "She made it!" Had I made it? All I could feel was the great, confused warmth of their energy inside myself, as if Christmas was once again what it used to be, a time of love. This year I had heard no canned music, struggled through no crowds, ridden on no suffocating elevators; what I did this year was enjoy Christmas before it happened.

They all went in a large confusion of suitcases, sewing machines, record players, hair dryers, and piles of clothes and skis.

Fathers said, "Do you really *have* to take all this stuff?" after four trips up and down stairs.

The rooms usually looked as if they had been stirred by a cyclone into an explosion of printed comforters, books, and clothes that flew through the air and landed on the floor, the chairs, the desks. Now the wild posters of motorcycle boys, the tender ones of loving couples embracing by the sea, and the pure psychedelic bursts of color hung upon the walls disconsolately, conveying nothing except a static vacuum, airless and dead. It was shockingly quiet. I walked down the first floor corridor, and peered in at untenanted rooms which were horribly dead and neat. No telephone ringing, no feet running. For some reason, I felt like crying. Did all this remind me of when my children left home?

It was still snowing and the house was full of the exaggerated absence of sound produced by heavy snows wrapping me in this enormous, empty place. Alone, one must be able to reach out and touch the walls on either side. I spent one night alone there, and the house moaned with strange creaks and thumps; I woke up every hour. I could not wait to get out; I was returned, with a shock, to being a woman alone. The Christmas tree was taken down and hauled out; Mrs. Perley came and made everything tidy. I made conversation.

"How did you do with that gardenia plant after Parent's Weekend?" Mrs. Perley was glad to take worn-out plants that drooped in the overheated house.

"It has buds all over it," she said, bustling around in her clean blue dress. I would not mind having Mrs. Perley close my eyes at the last. Shyly, she presented me a pine needle pillow covered with poinsettia cretonne, and it smelled fragrantly of the woods.

When Mrs. Perley had gone, with a cheerful "Merry Christmas!" I began to pack; it had been a long time since I felt such fear. I reminded myself that this was not like New York, where I was afraid to go out alone at night. And five in the afternoon had, for months, not been the cocktail hour that did not mean anything when one sat with a drink and no conversation. Five o'clock had become the time to go out in the hall, dressed for dinner, to talk, sometimes to hear that I "looked nice," sometimes later to be held up by girls as we skidded over the precarious ice to the Commons. But my ego was still fragile.

Was I ever to come to terms? A job was always an escape from the irreparable past, the past that could not be changed, fatal. What was the future? I could not imagine that it might be an improvement. What dismal thoughts to have after only one night alone! My hidden life was a long history of repression of unpleasant feelings; in these jungles I was lost, as if crisis after crisis had numbed my sense of direction and left me wondering, filled with a guilty terror, with a sense of loss that rose in my throat and choked me on a dark night. But this had been so when I was younger, when I could do something about it, something that might last, a new marriage, a new job.

I was lousy with literary quotes—"Trust thyself; every heart vibrates to that iron string." Books would not cure me; I was a gluttonous reader.

Packing now as fast as I could, I picked up a letter from my oldest grandson, signed, "Love Forever." Time now to give the hands of the clock a push, to get moving, to go on. Suddenly I felt compassion for older women who had no grandchildren, who, perhaps, didn't even like children—women who had lost their husbands, were too ill to go out, or too poor to enjoy what they had left. "We are all one creature," Colette said. For all I knew, some of the girls were going home to what they would

124

like to be free of; home would seem different now, except for a lucky few.

Absurdly enough, I was packing with my bedroom door locked. When I was ready, I opened the door and dragged my suitcases into the hall, trying to look at it as I had last August. Everything was somber, with the snow falling outside the windows in a thick veil flowing with wind. "Freedom is just another word for nothing left to lose," Janis Joplin sang. I had plenty to lose. The woman alone is afraid of death; the man alone also, if he is old. I had quite enough to lose before I came to that. Freedom! I could count one advantage of retirement; no alarm clock.

Staggering out into the small, narrow tunnel of the icy walk, I hauled my luggage into the car, wading and stumbling through three feet of snow, and was off to catch the Boston bus for Logan Airport—to my other Christmas in California with my children and grandchildren on December 25.

Descent into Purgatory

An unearthly quiet preceded the winter debacle known as mid-year exams. The tendency of the human race to huddle in times of crisis was never more concretely illustrated. Whereas in my day we went off to find solitude in some far corner of the library, these students congregated on the floor of the living room, which was now a shambles of skewed easy chairs, Kleenex, cigarette butts, discarded curlers, and, naturally, enough books to start a secondhand book store.

No one wore shoes any more, or slippers, either. The footgear was cast off, and at night I picked up loafers which were so stretched out at the sides that they resembled small gunboats, and put them two by two on the stairs. In some mysterious way, the feet got into the right pair on the way down the next morning.

Since desks and tables existed in the youthful mind only for the purpose of piling things on them, they were piled high for a week of camping. The student desk provided by the college wasn't big enough for even an industrious midget who owned a typewriter and ninety dollars worth of books, not to mention

126

paper, pencils, pens, typing ribbons, and fetishes like "Snoopy" or wacky dolls. Studying was now accomplished on the floor on one's belly, propped up on couches, or curled up in big chairs like cats. The feet were elevated. A few provident souls had acquired backrests (such as older ladies or invalids use in bed for reading) and had these stuck in corners. The whole living room was covered with arrangements for a siege, and once a girl had managed a stake-out, she left her books and other things (coffee mug, tissues, snacks, ash tray, pillows, blanket) there for the duration of the ordeal.

The dean of students happened by, looking neat, brown, and innocent. "My what a mess!" She was rewarded by disrespectful glares. The living room was a pigpen. To make matters worse, the electricity went off, and the grey light from the windows enhanced the scene of doom and melancholy. What was most depressing was that this state of affairs would go on, night and day, for a whole week.

Mrs. Perley walked in every morning, and did not attempt to clean the lower floor at all, since even the slightest noise was greeted with horrible scowls, and a loud "Shhhhhhhhhhhhhhh."

The first night of exams I began the nightly feeding, a custom inspired by those who stayed up all night and were sometimes observed at five in the morning, fast asleep, bent over a book, but still sitting upright like limp rag dolls. Maria told me one morning that she slept on the floor part of the night, but her "daughter" came and put a blanket over her and a pillow under her head. Her "daughter" was Les, otherwise called "Little Myrtle" by Maria, and Maria was "Big Myrtle." I reflected that Les was a thoughtful soul, for I remembered her with Lisa. Maria enlivened the study scene by putting on a long sick red wig. "It matches my skin," she said. A girl named Jenny, who believed in humor and comfort, was wearing a red Dr. Denton sleeping suit, a red jockey cap, and dangling gold earrings; now and then she flourished a baton. Jenny was worried about getting into Boston University, but this did not dampen her spirits.

In the autumn, I had been instructed by the dean to use some funds provided by the college for the purpose of having the freshmen in to tea, but a great cry arose, "Save the money for exam week!" At ten o'clock in the evening when we had our usual thirty minutes of riot, I had the food ready. We had English muffins toasted, with honey, cinnamon and sugar, or peanut butter and jelly. I melted a whole pound of butter. We had a box of MacIntosh apples, and a percolator full of hot water for instant tea or coffee. I never got thanked so profusely in my life, not even when I laid on a full-course dinner that took days to prepare. There was munching and crunching and smacking. The eating orgy soon developed into acrobatics. Barbie rode people around piggy-back, and she got Legs on her back, then flipped her over her head with Legs screaming. They tried the pile-up trick and the pyramid.

The next morning I woke up in a murky, rainy grey fog suitable for a Hitchcock murder. The electricity was off again. Only Maria was up. She hadn't undressed all night, and she helped me gather up jackets, loafers, blankets, books, notebooks destined after exams for the trash barrel. Then she ran around calling everyone who had an exam at eight o'clock. My spirits lifted slightly when I saw how much care they took of each other.

Mrs. Perley arrived. "The roads are solid ice," she said. She gave me some homemade raspberry jelly and some apple jelly. I opened them; both smelled of walking through orchards of fruit blossoms in spring.

Girls came running down the stairs and skidded down the walks dressed in pants, jackets, fancy flowered rain hats, straw hats with feathers, and no make-up at all. The hats were the only indication that this was not a day of national mourning.

I walked down the first floor corridor and saw on one of the doors, "Although there are some things in this world more wonderful than sexual intercourse, there is nothing *exactly like it*."

I didn't make it to the studio that morning. A girl named Fannie appeared at my door and said she wanted to talk about her English. I had never before had any conversation with Fannie, who was a shy blonde, wispy; I had seen Fannie sitting on the lap of her boy friend, Merton. Appearances in Fannie's case *were* deceiving. While she seldom spoke, she was not averse to rolling on the floor with Merton, as if life were one long hot and heavy wrestling match.

"I want to compare and contrast *King Lear* with one of the Greek tragedies, with appropriate examples, and we will have a writing time of one hour. The exam is tomorrow and this is only half of it," she said in a small voice, nervously pushing her hair behind her ears.

Christ in the Mountains, I thought. The faculty must be *mad*. What was this, Radcliffe?

But Fannie had, after all, never come to me before.

"You could take Cordelia and Antigone," I said, no doubt overcome by my former ruthless practice of pushing them to the brink at exam times. She smiled and ran off.

In the afternoon, I made it over to the studio; when I got there, I thanked God I would never have to take a final exam again, except the one of giving up this life. Next door in the basement, a girl had fixed up a card table in the center of the kitchen, and she was ensconced for the week. She deserved high marks for survival fitness; not only did she get down and grab this quiet place for herself early in the game, but she sang while she studied. Sometimes she fell silent. Did she sing when she was stumped or when she was finding the solution?

I had two crickets down there, too. One was spending the winter in the boiler room and one somewhere in a crack in my bathroom. They both chirped their songs and then there was silence; the one in the bathroom seemed to imagine the sound of a typewriter might be coming from still another cricket.

I thought about what the purpose of education really was. I couldn't help thinking that for Les to put a blanket and pillow down for Maria the night before had something to do with it. Pale, white little Les with her long hair like Eve's had fixed up for herself a nice house under the grand piano where she studied with a big vari-colored woolen pillow. When I happened by, she would say, "Would you like coffee or tea?" as if she were playing house.

"I would like a very dry vodka martini on the rocks with an olive and no lemon."

Les poured from an imaginary bottle into the invisible glass and stirred. She looked precisely ten years old.

"It's perfect," I said. "My, but you do make a wonderful martini."

In the evening Maria came in and sat on the floor of my sitting room with her roommate, a most proper Vermonter named Helvetia Perkins. They wanted to talk about *Moby-Dick*. I wondered if it was because Maria was black that she found the White Whale a villain to her taste. She had other reasons, all of them good.

"Hating is like the Black Panthers," she said. We read aloud the great, rolling sea waves of Melville's prose, and Maria sparkled for joy.

"Isn't that great! Wow!" she yelled. She remembered every single thing about the book, the things I had forgotten since I took American Lit., Queequeg's tattoos and Perth's suicidal life. She knew Ishmael was the seeker. "What was Don Quixote seeking?" she asked.

"A better world where there were gallant knights who rescued people in distress. But everyone thought he was crazy, an impossible dreamer."

"That's me. I'm going to write my exam about the quest— Ahab's quest was from hatred and destruction because he hurt. I am going to write about my quest. We are supposed to write about what *Moby-Dick* means to us in the world of today." Maria was all alight; her vivid mind was glowing.

Helvetia, who was tight-lipped, thin, pale, said nothing. But they were ideal roommates; they had free speech without quarreling, and lived together with a policy of laissez-faire.

When Maria moved toward the fine points of *Moby-Dick*, Helvetia kicked a book that was patently a "review trot" and said with disdain, "I'll bet you are getting your ideas out of *that*." Vermonters do their own thinking. But Maria was too excited to pay any attention.

"I am crazy about this book. Melville thought an American could do what Shakespeare did."

"Humph," said Helvetia.

130

The Little Red Devil

In college some people get names they do not have in the outside world, names that stick forever in the minds of their classmates, never to be used by anyone else. In some instances this is the last time in a girl's life she is called by her surname. Thus Eugenia Chace was called Chace, and Emily Tuttle, Barbie's roommate, was merely Tuttle. There were other inexplicable variations; Kimberly Jones, who was slim, pretty, and wide-eyed, was called Artichoke and Artie for short. I couldn't find out what inspired this goofy name; perhaps it had something to do with hair rollers. No one ever told me how these monikers evolved, or why other girls were Margaret, June, or Dorothy.

The name game was contagious, and I called the girls whatever I heard most of the time. I was not able to call the beautiful, gentle Beatrice of the black eyes and dusky hair by the name of *Balls*. But when a girl bellowed, *"Balls!"* up the stairs, the boys who waited below took on a curious and suppressed look of disbelief. What the girls called me, I didn't know, for in my presence they addressed me politely.

Next door to Tuttle and Barbie was the room of Chace and Britt. Britt was really Elaine Britton; she was the wildest of the lot, with quantities of red hair and a face like a pale O. Chace and Britt lived in a sty, where their clothes were thrown on the floor every time they undressed, and sometimes they slept on bare mattress ticking; I suppose they were too wild and forgetful to walk down to the basement once a week to obtain some clean sheets. They were both extremely vocal when no adults were in sight, and never entered the house without sound effects ranging from curses to importunate wails, howls, and shrieks. No event in life was too small to merit an expression of their considerable lung power.

Britt had an unadulterated distrust of everyone who appeared to be an aged wreck unable to have anything to say to her. She called me "Mrs. Miller" for months, and never talked to me, but rushed through the house like a small, red-eyed cyclone, reeking of burnt rope. She was stoned most of the time. She repaired to a fraternity house on most evenings and all weekends, so I did not see much of her although I heard her. She was swinging, day and night, between two worlds, and everyone liked this; Britt provided the whole house with a vicarious sensation of abandon and devil-may-care dissipation. Dullness was not in her, but self-destruction was. I saw her always as reeling, out of balance, like a character in an avant garde film, weary of life before she was twenty, searching and not finding, unable to sit down or relax, or to study for very long. Her parents were spending the winter in southern France and were never available.

During exam week Britt studied with her security blanket; it was a fuzzy white rug. She looked desolate, day after day, but believed she could cram enough into her head to make up for a whole semester of doing nothing in the way of academic pursuits.

I saw Britt as an abandoned child. When she came in late, bedraggled and swearing, she would go to the room of Phyllis and Rose, comfortable people, and wrap herself in a rug in the middle of the floor between their beds. She was one of the "desperate ones," but she had such pride. One Sunday after-

132

noon in the fall, Britt and Lisa were going up the stairs, and Britt was saying, "What happened last night? *Shit*. Did she get torn up?"

Lisa refused to say. I could picture Lisa, with her pointed features and skinny frame, looking rather like an amusing fox, beside fierce little Britt. Their steps faded away.

My thoughts drifted as I sat there not reading the *Times*, and I remembered that Britt got herself rather torn up one night, sometime before the bus from Dartmouth got back at two in the morning. The campus police appeared at the back door and said, "One girl is running around outside and does not know what building she belongs in."

Several girls dashed out the back door. They knew it was Britt. I was standing in the middle of the hall in my bathrobe, feeling anxious, when Britt stumbled in the front door, wringing wet and barefoot, her hair hanging in red wet strings, her face pale as a white plate. She did not recognize me. After huddling over the sign-out book, trembling, and managing to sign in with water dripping on the book, she stumbled past me and upstairs. In that moment, I saw that her eyes were dilated and unseeing. She never found her shoes.

At that time, Britt was having nothing to do with me, but a little later on she did. She had violated so many of the lenient rules that our house council campused her for a whole weekend. She was a frantic, wild bird caged, flying through the house, up, down, in and out. On Saturday night I heard crashing sounds in the basement under me, and went down. Britt was standing in a sea of broken glass in the kitchen.

My reaction to hysteria is always freezing, withdrawal, numbness; this is *my* hysteria, my terror, my fear of violence—violence buried so long in myself that when it erupts, I become savage with words, like a shrew. But I could not let it erupt now. We stared at each other in silence. Britt was a forlorn child, but a child so angry that a touch would drive her away forever. The little kitchen, drab and gloomy, lit by a single glaring bulb, held in its walls the commonplace—the old refrigerator, the metal sink, the Coke machine—but the floor held murder that gradually came up like poison gas, tear gas to my eyes.

I stared a long time at Britt, who returned the stare, a wild bird confronting a cat. I went from numbness to fear to naivete to homely words. "Come on, I'll help you clean it up."

Gradually, the fear receded, as we took the broom and dustpan and began to sweep up glass, which was a glittering icy carpet all over the floor, splinters, shards, chunks, some of it swimming in dark bloody Coke. Had she put money in the machine to get more bottles to break? As we began to sweep, Britt turned into a helpless, willing child, holding the dustpan, but saying nothing. As we worked, the tension subsided. "The girls come down in their bare feet," I said, pushing the broom as far as I could under the refrigerator, into the corners, "and they will get cut if we don't get up all the little pieces." The glass glittered with blue lights and sharp points. Britt did not answer, and I felt I was in a mad world. When we finished, the wastebasket was full of broken glass right up to the top.

"How about coming upstairs and watching television with me?" She nodded her head, and walked up the stairs behind me. We sat quietly. Now and then she looked at me with questioning glances, a naughty little girl. The TV was quacking away. It was a strange evening, for we did not speak. We were caught in congealed emotions—fear and anger. I do not know, even now, why I could not talk to Britt then.

When she got up and left me, I put a sign in the kitchen not to walk there in bare feet, and Mrs. Perley said the next morning, "What on earth happened in the kitchen last night? There was glass *everywhere*, tiny slivers of it."

Not many days after this, I heard terrifying yells, screams, and thumps coming from my sitting room, ordinarily inviolate except by my permission. I went in to find Leslie rolling on the floor and shrieking because Britt was eating my African violet. Britt sat with my little plant in her hand, looking as if she had discovered a new and succulent form of salad.

This time I was furious, but decided to assume the stance of an attendant in a mental hospital; I presume this is one of nonsurprise. Stony-faced, I took my African violet and inspected it, as Britt and Les rolled around in a tangle of pantlegs. Britt had consumed several leaves and pulled out one part of the plant by the roots. Both girls were laughing hysterically.

"I wanted to make Les blow her mind," Britt said, as if this were the most reasonable aim in the world.

"The poor plant. It is a living thing, you know," I remarked in a cold anger. I was beginning to learn that what worked was never to appear shocked. In spite of the fact that I have smashed dishes in preference to hitting a person, I have never eaten an African violet; their leaves are a bit hairy-looking for my taste. Quite seriously, I realized that Britt was beyond anything I knew how to do for her; she would keep on until she got hurt. She invited punishment.

During exam week, the rebels repaired to the out-of-doors at intervals; they told me they kept their beer in the woods. Now as I write, drinking is "legal" on campus after one is twenty; drinking will never be the same again—imagine having your beer fresh out of a snowbank on a moonlit evening in a wintry wood, especially if you should be studying! And what happened when it snowed over the beer? The whole expedition must have turned into a scrabbling treasure hunt, with Tuttle and Chace gasping like thirsty explorers in a desert.

Tuttle had a pair of Alaska paratrooper boots of white canvas about five sizes too large for her. She wore them with miniskirts and navy pantyhose; the boots were tied around her slender legs and made her look childlike. When she walked, she moved with big white flippers.

One day, Britt ran in, screaming with pain, sat down on the floor, and rocked back and forth, moaning and yelping like an injured puppy.

"My feet are frostbitten," she moaned. She had tried wearing the canvas boots in the snow with nothing but her bare feet inside. Tuttle was very calm and ran some cool water for Britt to put her feet in. They were soon back to normal.

The winter forays into the woods continued. "I never really got to *know* Chace," Les said, "until the night we were drinking beer over in the bushes by the president's house, and we ended up holding each other off the ground while we went to the bathroom." My mind boggled with wonder as I imagined this scene in several feet of snow.

✶

When we had outlasted exam week, we had a week of recovery known as "Semester Break." Almost everyone went home. A great ice storm produced showers of jeweled bits from the trees and pistol shots as the ice hit the ground; icicles loosened and fell like daggers. When the sun came out, the campus took on an uncanny, wild glitter. Whole branches broke from trees.

When I was ready to leave for a vacation and had locked my door, a few girls who were staying here to ski scampered through the hall, among them, Britt. For several days we had been avoiding each other because of a little scene we had one morning at five o'clock, when she woke me by loud talking. "I'm sorry," she said then, with fake politeness.

"*You are not,*" I almost shouted, causing Britt to look as if her nursemaid had suddenly developed paranoia. Being patient all the time is lethal, I said to myself, in a feeble self-justification. Now she looked rather like Puck, small, frail, in blue cotton shorts and a thin white shirt, with her hair hanging in rough strings.

I sat down on the settle in my coat and fur hat and told her I was sorry. "Kiss and make up," one of the girls said, so I got up and put my arms around Britt's neck and kissed her cheek.

"I like you, Britt." To my surprise, she had tears glistening. "Do you really?"

"Yes, I really do."

"I like you, too. You are like Tuttle, real cool. You are both cynics. But I can respect anyone who is honestly angry."

This was the first time I had ever been called a cynic; if I were, how could I have trusted those rascals?

The other girls vanished, satisfied with their peacemaking, and Britt sat down in the middle of the hall floor. I took off my hat and sat there wondering, What next? But Britt just sat there, a cross-legged pixie. I tried to level with her.

136

"You have a great zest for life—you are really *alive*. An older person feels 'not with it' compared to you."

Britt ignored this. She looked perplexed, younger than she was. "I want to talk about writing. I've had two or three feelings in my whole life that I have total recall about, and I want to write about them. They were beautiful feelings."

I sighed. "Do you have any images for them?"

She looked even more puzzled. She waited.

"An image is something like that young girl standing in the sea in Joyce's *Portrait of the Artist*—you had to read that, didn't you? The girl looking like a beautiful sea bird, and she meant beauty to Joyce." What a lousy explanation of the epiphany!

Britt just sat there, thinking this over.

I wanted very much to leave, and I wanted to explain to Britt that she was self-destructive and talking about "beautiful feelings" was not the point. This was the first time Britt had ever come to me in a mood to discuss anything at all.

But in the middle of this, Maria and Les came storming through the hall in one of their domestic fetes. Maria was yelling, "Daughter, daughter, dauauauauaughter" at the top of her voice, and it resounded through the almost empty house. Les tore upstairs, and called in a dulcet tone, "Mother, are you downstairs?" I was momentarily distracted by these playhouse activities, for I remembered that Les had a "Shit List" on her door, and one of the names on it was *Mother*.

Now Britt, with a memory of "beautiful feelings," sat in the middle of the hall rug, and I remembered hearing her say, "Jesus Christ, I'll never forgive myself." Somehow this stuck in my memory as the real Britt. Outside the ice was breaking, cracking, falling.

We could not hold onto the moment. Les came running downstairs with a bottle of turpentine and said she could not get the top off and she wanted to paint. Could she borrow my pliers? I had to unlock my door to get the pliers.

"Don't burn the house down smoking while you are using turpentine," I said.

Then Britt picked up my suitcase and said she wanted to escort me to the car, over solid ice and snow in her bare feet and summer garments, but I wouldn't let her. The ice was so slippery that before I could leave, it took six girls to push my car and get it started.

As I left, with the door open and the bitter wind blowing back Britt's hair, I looked back and said, "Do you think you are going to make your grades?"

She shook her head. "But I think they'll let me stay until the end of the year."

Britt was wrong. Perhaps one of her most distinguishing characteristics was that she imagined things would turn out well when everything was all set to be otherwise. I was away during that week when Britt's chickens came home to roost, but I came back for one day in a feathery snowstorm to get a dress for a dinner party. The snow blew so wildly over the ice that I was careful to park where I wouldn't need to be pushed. I saw Britt's station wagon with the flower symbols on it.

When I went into the dorm, it was weirdly silent, with a few girls making distant little noises like mice in the walls. And when I went back out, Britt had moved her car and was scraping the ice off the windshield. She came over and we talked through the whistling wind.

As we talked, she applied her icescraper to my windshield with unaccustomed consideration. She seemed too subdued.

"Have you been skiing?"

"No, I've been home to see my parents. They are back for a while. They have a puppy they treat like a child," she said irrelevantly. But I wondered about the connection. Did they treat Britt like a person or a puppy? When I left her, she was standing in the whirling snow and wind in her chopped-off jeans, looking wistful.

This was the last time I saw Britt. When the semester break was over, a Queen Anne table had been broken and one leg lay in the hall. Mrs. Perley and I had a chat about this. "They must have had a big party," she said. "Everything was at sixes and sevens, and there was cocoa on the rug. And the table was lying there just like that." I called Ben, our fix-it man. "They would

138

have had to *stand* on it," he said, shaking his head. "That was a very sturdy table. And where is the other leg?" We searched everywhere, but the leg had totally disappeared.

Rose came out in the hall and said mournfully, "Britt was kicked out."

"Where is the table leg?"

"It got broken."

"Did Britt break it?"

She just smiled and turned away. They all loved her as if she were the primitive part of themselves, the one who did not find it in her to obey reason. They spoke of her now as of someone who had died. "Poor Britt."

The mystery of the missing table leg persisted, for we could not have the table repaired without it; it was a nicely turned, very old Queen Anne leg. She wanted us to blow our minds again. I never did know the real Britt. I had only caught glimpses now and then of her despair, her energy, her revolt, and finally, her sweetness. Not once did she come to me for sympathy, or for anything else, until it was too late.

I find that one change that came with being a little older was that I could not give to the young a philosophical explanation about *anything*. Such maneuvers turned grey in the face of a storm of tears over an F on a term paper by someone whom the life force never meant to write about the Greek theatre.

The next night at dinner I told Mrs. Wyckoff about the missing table leg, and she said, "Did they have a fire in the fireplace while you were away?" Of course. In the morning I asked Mrs. Perley the same question. She stopped running the vacuum cleaner and laughed. "I told you they had quite a bash on Monday night—remember? And they did have a fire in the fireplace, and the table leg is probably gone forever."

I could imagine this vividly. Britt was desolate, and she broke the table in a fit of rage, and they consoled her by adding to the outburst. I could see the table leg burning and crackling away and everyone laughing. But what I imagine is not always correct; it merely consoles *me*.

A good old well-turned Queen Anne leg! Semester break indeed. Sometimes their sense of humor was subtle.

I did not forget Britt. She could "respect anyone who was honestly angry." One evening we looked at "Snoopy," who was up to all kinds of devilment because Linus sent him off to obedience school for a refresher course; when he came back, he was just as bad as ever and broke his leash, licked Lucy's face until she yelled, "I give up!" and then he raced around like a crazy dog.

This reminded me of Britt. I mourned Britt and I wished she could come back. When Barbie came in, we both mourned Britt and I said to Barbie, "Do you know what Britt did last year? Miss Barnes told me. Britt went over to the drug store and bought some birth control pills and told the druggist she was sent to buy them for her house mother, Miss Twickley, and she signed the slip and got away with it."

Barbie collapsed and slapped the side of her jeans twice, something she does when she is delighted beyond words. We all miss Britt; she was the part of ourselves we cannot show, the little red devil.

Chace, who had somehow acquired Britt's original birth announcement, posted this on her door beside a print of an old-fashioned mother with a huge, bawling child. The caption said, "What's a mother to do?"

The Toothbrush Trick

When January was over, my spirits lifted. We had survived the lowest point in the year, when Nature almost commanded us to stop, fold up, and sleep. February was the academic Second Chance. The dorm was very quiet, even when the boys came in to call. Everyone was studying conscientiously, and the girls who made the Dean's List were being congratulated. The freshmen, of whom six were on probation, were sober and seemed to realize for the first time that to make the Dean's List was an achievement more to be desired than winning the hockey or basketball championship.

The president started off the new semester with a convocation address which was a marvel of wit and wisdom. Afterwards, he opened the meeting, and the same old questions were asked. Why do the girls have to attend the concerts on Saturday nights? (We never would have, either.) Could they have trimesters? Could they have a winter vacation and go out to work in the world? Could they have boys visit them in their rooms? Education is a fluid thing with infinite variations in new experiments, as if the outer plans could create the inner peace—and the essence of education is that it will never be at peace, for it is a quest, something closely related to the word *question*. The girls' questions were prophetic.

In northern California spring always came in February, when the winter rains stopped pouring down and the acacias blew their golden blossoms everywhere; the Japanese iris came up, the daffodils nodded, and the Daphne shrub bloomed with its poignant, sweet scent. The pussy willows came out in soft catkins down by the Bolinas waters, and the air took on a clear shining without smog. So for me February was still spring, and I imagined the black and white filigrees of birches had a different look of sap within them. The dogs were playing in the snow wildly, barking and tussling. The sun was shining in brilliance, going in and out behind the clouds, capricious, dazzling.

All I heard from the girls, however, was the winter doldrums. "I really don't like anybody." People complained. Ellen said everyone was taking her food without asking, and her records, too. Other people said it was Ellen's own fault; that she exuded a feeling of unlimited supplies and everyone else was broke. Pat said that people sat in her room and talked when she wanted to go to bed, and that Legs would not turn in a single paper unless Pat read it first. Going to Dartmouth had become "boring," I heard over and over again.

We had meetings to air our gripes, which were manifold. Barbie sighed, "I never knew human nature was so complicated! I wish we could get some of the complainers out of our room so we could *breathe!*"

The invasion of Private Territory became a continuous theme. It was like a Hydra with nine heads, and two grew where one was cut off. It baffled me how to convey to the girls whatever it was that made me protect my own territory; was this a question of age? Not entirely, for some children loathe having interruptions, and some ladies like to have the neighbors running in and out. Without awareness of a need for solitude, I would have had constant companionship.

The girls complained about the continuous borrowing, but they continued to permit it. Some borrowing from me was valid: a martini pitcher for a play prop, a hammer, a pair of

142

pliers, some cough syrup. But upstairs it was different. People wanted to play their records and found the cases empty, missed ski jackets and sweaters (which were not really stolen, for they were easily found), and looked for their snacks only to find they had been eaten up by room prowlers.

But the worst was the borrowing of precious time. We could tell now which girls would become women who dote on morning kaffee klatsches that take up hours, go to lunches and teas on every possible occasion, talk on the phone in between, and tell their husbands all the problems of the day before dinner. Some of them even decided to sleep in someone else's bed without notice.

The girls were remarkably long-suffering with friends who suffered from a dependency syndrome, and they went on pouring out sympathy and attention. Barbie and Tuttle tried almost everything. Since Barbie was house president, she was fair game. The custom of the dorm was to put a shoe on the doorknob if you did not want company, but the People-Eaters opened the door and walked in anyway. That year the Drama Department put on a play, *The Delicate Balance* by Edward Albee, which showed what happened to a family when they admitted some friends to stay indefinitely because the friends said, "We are afraid." Barbie and Tuttle had too much character to put up with these invasions forever. They managed to climb up through a trapdoor into the attic, where they found an immensely heavy old chain that would be murderous in the hands of a criminal, and they hung it over their door in a nice, even loop. The People-Eaters crawled under it. Barbie said, "I give up."

One evening I was calmly reading a Simenon—thank God for Simenon when one is prevented from imagining anything beyond being snowbound—when I heard a series of yells upstairs rapidly rising into a chorus of hysterics. I often ignored these demonstrations, for screaming is as necessary to the young feminine psyche as crying is to babies, but the uproar continued for so long that I went out, thinking that perhaps an unknown male had invaded the upper regions. I saw ten heads peering over the bannister, and in unison the heads shouted with fury,

"Someone has stolen all our toothbrushes!!"Then there was silence.

Brandie said, "*You* took our toothbrushes." Brandie was a thin, owl-eyed girl with short hair who was never in trouble; she had an English wit and sense of fair play. And Kate, who was so thin and severe, the pre-med from Maine, said, "You did take our toothbrushes, didn't you?" I had become quite fond of Kate. All ten pairs of eyes waited for the answer, but I was speechless. Even if Mrs. Perley took things out of the bathrooms when they were left out on the washbasins, she would scarcely invade everyone's room and confiscate toothbrushes kept where they were supposed to be.

Kate said, "Someone even went into *my* bathroom and took *my* toothbrush." Kate was one of the few who had a private bathroom left over from the days of a chaperone on each floor.

I couldn't help laughing. There hadn't been such mass panic since the night they pulled down all the blinds because they heard that some madman had strangled five girls in a junior college on the East coast—a rumor that turned out to be false. Mellie, a valued adviser on the first floor, said she knew nothing about a plot to take toothbrushes to "prove a point." What point? But no one on the first floor had lost her toothbrush.

Barbie called a meeting to discuss the Honor Code, which had two chief tenets: one reported herself when she broke the rules, and one spoke to anyone else who had broken the rules and advised her to report herself to the Honor Board. I felt sure the lost toothbrushes would appear.

"But how will we know which is our toothbrush?"

"Don't you know your own toothbrush?"

"Well, lots of them will be the same."

A quandary indeed.

"Maybe someone is trying to break up the winter doldrums." The voice of common sense.

The toothbrushes appeared the next evening, dangling from strings all across Chace's room, and she ran around looking clownish, saying, "I didn't do it!" I went up to see the toothbrush display. It was one of the funniest things I have ever seen—dozens of toothbrushes hanging in a great display of pop art,

144

their plastic handles gleaming in the light. Everyone was howling with glee.

As it turned out, only a gang could have executed the Toothbrush Trick. Barbie came around to see me; she was so delighted that she resembled a St. Bernard puppy. Her hands were waving, and when she sat down, she wriggled with delight.

"I had no idea they would be so *mad,*" she said. Barbie never expected anyone to act neurotic.

"You are a rascal."

"Chace and Tuttle and I did it. We think it is time to terrorize the dorm, and we were planning a whole series of things like putting masking tape over the outside of Kate's door so she would walk into it while she is asleep. This place needs a little livening up."

It may be that Barbie brought the sun out.

"Last year some kids filled our room up to the ceiling with crumpled newspapers, and it took them four hours to do it. I came home and opened the door, so I waited until Tuttle came. She was kind of drunk, and she walked right into it in the dark. Wow! Well, we dug it out and until we could get into our beds we slept in there like two little hamsters in their nests."

I perceived the first signs of spring fever, which must begin deep down at the time when the bulbs are putting forth their first shoots underground. The old college prank is better than taking things so seriously that the whole campus must be terrorized until the authorities have to call in the state police. I almost wished the boys would go back to panty raids.

The spring of 1970 was going to be unforgettable, but I did not know that then.

When Icicles Hang by the Wall

Spring fever! Ridiculous in the wake of the greatest nor'
easter I could ever have imagined. One Sunday morning we
awoke to a scene of gusting snow and wind. The drifts were
piled up outside my window until I could scarcely see out, and
the screens were blotted with snow. The men could not plow
fast enough to keep the walks clear, but they tried, over and
over again; then the snow blew over the walks again to a depth
of several feet.

The storm came as stealthily as a white panther, creeping
up for several days with lazy, deceptive ease. Around four
o'clock on Sunday I was frightened, for the dark had set in with
alarming speed.

By five o'clock, the girls were returning from their weekend at the Dartmouth Winter Carnival. They came in stamping
and blowing.

"Whew. Did you have a good time? Did you get laid?"

"Oh, he was awful. I am going to give up boys *forever*."
(Whispers.) "I almost went out of my mind."

"I have so much *work* to do!"

146

"My date was groovy." (More whispers).

"Well, she slept on the floor of my room and brought in all her clothes and everything."

We heard sudden, ear-splitting screams, repeated over and over like the dying statements of someone who has just been stabbed twelve times in the back. I began to run around like a distracted hen.

"Never mind. It is only Maria. Maybe Les is beating her up or something." The mother-daughter game seemed to be more complicated with Maria and Les than "role playing."

Connection in my head! Maria did not go to the Winter Carnival. Why not? She spent all her weekends at Dartmouth . . . nearly always.

"I'm going to wash my hair," Pat, our practical member, remarked. This was always the solution to everything.

By nine o'clock we were watching the Royal Shakespeare Company do a "mod" version of *Midsummer Night's Dream*. In the warm room away from the increasing violence outdoors, the girls snuggled in blankets on the floor. The steam heat sent up suffocating dry warmth as Puck and the fairies vied with Quince, Bottom, Starveling, and Snout. Periodically, the door opened.

"Angie can't make it back. Shall I make out an overnight permission?"

Barbie came in. "I want to see Simon and Garfunkel on the Fred Astaire show and everyone downstairs is looking at 'Spartacus.'". We obligingly switched channels. Fred was dancing. "Gosh, isn't he cool? He must be at least sixty-five." Then we sighed through Simon and Garfunkel as they sang "Scarborough Fair" in the coolest possible tones. Virgie said, "They get me in my guts." Virgie, who was in love, had changed from her former boisterous self into a languishing maiden.

Legs was doing front hall duty and got up every time the phone rang. Her grey V-necked sweater had nothing on under it, but she was wearing pendant earrings, and her cheeks were very pink. She looked as sweet and delicate as a Dresden shepherdess.

By the time we were thinking about going to bed, the white

panther was howling out his white rage, and the whole campus was scourged by a thrashing fury. Barbie said she had had a good time at the Carnival with the boy who sent her funny post cards—Barbie preferred the outdoor type who hiked, skied and wasn't too lecherous. But Barbie was earthy, a lusty girl who had talents which she never let me see or hear; an informant said Barbie ran around upstairs bare to the waist, with her ample bosoms bobbing. Downstairs, however, Barbie dressed in a long blue robe; she had a sense of the fitness of things, what to do when and where. She had a way of curling her lip that kept her from looking too sweet, and a capricious sense of humor.

The next morning the storm was so wild that the phone rang and announced there would be NO CLASSES TODAY! So everyone got out of bed as if by communication in sleep and ran around yelling for joy.

"Let's have a party!"

"Do you have anything to eat?" I asked.

"We are going to make maple syrup candy in the snow."

Rae said, "It feels kind of funny in my stomach with only crackers and cheese."

I wondered what maple syrup would do to her stomach.

The TV announced that this was the greatest mauling the East had had in many a long year, but we were snug inside except for Rae, who had a window loose from its frame.

I called Mr. Rufus, the head custodian. He growled, "Can't they put it back in?"

"Yes, but it won't stay."

"O.K. I'll send someone over with a nail."

This was a crusty reminder that if I had any New England gumption, I would have produced a nail myself. "For want of a nail"—*that* didn't happen to a *woman* in the old rhyme, Mr. Rufus.

My car was completely snowed under, and when Mr. Rufus plowed, it would be buried on all sides so that we would not get it out for days. The sun peered down fitfully, but by afternoon the sky became an uncompromising, surging grey. By lunch time, we had become *really hungry* and I was escorted over to the commons by a brace of girls who promised to pull

148

me up if I blew down. When we passed the art center, which had snow almost to the top of its plate glass windows, a girl's head was peeking over the top of a drift. At the same time, a head appeared through a snow tunnel, like a mole coming out from underground.

That afternoon they all turned into snow animals. Mellie, with her long legs and scarf flying, dived straight through drifts like a surfer in ocean waves. Joseph Wood Krutch says that only winter is sublime, is pure, is detached from man; but he should have seen this. Rose and Phyllis were out wading like enormous bears, lumbering their legs up and down, swinging on tree branches until they fell in the deep snow. Rose's fur hat came down over her eyes, and she laughed. The whole front campus was a mass of churned-up ice cream where hundreds of girls wallowed and swallowed and rolled. Les and Mellie showered snow all over the hall. Les had on her yellow oilskin jacket and pants, which were big enough for a paunchy man.

"Oh, we had so much fun! We found a real mountain of snow, bigger than anything, and we dived in it!" There was so much snow in the hall that someone cried, "I'm going to make an angel on the floor," and there was a flopping on backs, with arms and legs waving.

In the middle of all this, and with rock going over my head, I felt cozy and fell asleep. It is still inexplicable how I could sleep in the center of this unconscionable noise, but there it was. Life was going on with unabated zest; I sometimes wondered if we were all going to blow up in an enormous explosion of sheer energy. The girls never complained about a violent change in the weather; they rolled in snow, and in the spring, they sat on the grass with their skirts spread out like petals, pretending they were flowers. If it was hot, they went swimming, and if it rained, they ran in it until they were soaked. What they did with the weather was immerse themselves in it.

This was not a week; it was a nor'easter—the second blast followed the first. My car turned into a little white hippo with big eyes. Nap time. Someone was singing in the hall, "Maybe a rich man/ maybe a rich man. . . ." The sandpaper of soles on the stairs going up—the thunkety-thunk on the stairs coming down. The clump-clump overhead. The back door moaned heavily; the front door bumped. The plumbing groaned. I fell asleep to some whistling music, and dreamed about my brothers mowing the grass with an old-fashioned gentle lawnmower that provided an accompaniment to dreaming.

When I was resting on my bed, I heard rock music. Sometimes it was music like a big, groaning vacuum sweeper which unaccountably had the power to wheeze its way up and down the scale to a regular beating and thumping of small wooden sticks, to a whirring of silver wires, clunking out and resuming again in a frenzy of whines and yells.

Then there was music like burps from the belly of a Lilliputian whale, or the squeezed guts of an accordion; all of it merging in a rocking motion, that sway and stomp called *rock*. And rock will get into you, if you listen long enough; rock is seductive of blood and bone; rock is feet and hands and the beat of a heart; rock is a great, bead-swinging motion, back and forth on a marimba, with a bear grunting on a tuba.

I began to get inside of rock music; this was surprising. I thought formerly that rock got inside of anyone who understood it, and that perhaps no one could understand it unless he got up on his feet and rocked his body. It was Lisa who got me up to the third floor one Saturday night to a "dress up" party. I got out a Hawaiian mumu and big straw hat to wear, but as I climbed the stairs, I heard rock blasting. Lisa, by turning herself into an enthusiastic coaxing teacher, got me by slow degrees into dancing to rock. "It's good for your arthritis!" she yelled; she was right.

I had forgotten that soft rocking is how we put babies to sleep, and rocking is very soothing. I was afflicted with a prejudice against hard rock anyway, but by 1970 rock had become softer, and I went to sleep and woke up feeling the sound swaying and myself inside a thin bubble. A guitar was gently ascending and descending the stairsteps of chords. Soft rock is often about love, about silence, about sounds as gentle as those of leaves coming down, or rain. I couldn't hear the words, so it was the music that was swaying through the walls and the ceiling, not too loudly. Sometimes one of the girls was singing along with the record; and I came to understand why they loved this music, but I am no more able to explain this than they were. Either you are inside with them, or you are outside without them. The girls were compassionate; they came to understand that a female who, in 1912, was singing "Jesus wants me for a sunbeam," had problems. Rock had become a battering ram, a culture assault, a road map; to me it became more than a noise, a jolt; it became change of consciousness.

I had no sooner noted the above and gone over to dinner than my feeble pride took a fall. The Student Government had provided a stereo for the dinner hour, and it was blaring "hot rock" that fairly shook my back teeth and landed a series of belts to my stomach. No one at the adults' table could make himself heard without shouting, so I forgot myself and got up and turned down the stereo to medium. For this I was hissed and booed. I am sure the girls from my dorm were embarrassed for me. The adults then held a conference and decided to move to a table at the farthest corner of the commons for the dinner hour.

In the commons, the adults comprised about twenty-five people and the girls six hundred, so we were a minority group. But it seemed to me that we were settling most of our problems by moving out of the way, and since we had been doing this for a long time (with feeble and emotional protests) it was no wonder that the younger generation expected it.

The Haliburtons were house residents who brought Jimmy, their year-old baby, to the dining room, and his high chair was right in front of the stereo; when they sat him down, he began to cry. His parents moved his high chair around to the side of the table, but he remained cross throughout the meal, and at one point began screaming. The Haliburtons were under thirty, and they did not mind commotion from the stereo, but Jimmy's father, who was working on a Ph.D. from Dartmouth, got up and went to lean over in the baby's face to yell, "STOP SCREAMING!" The baby left off screaming and began to cry again.

The wild colors and exaggerated sounds preferred by the

151

college generation suggested to me that their senses were jaded by noise and harsh colors. Mellie said it "eased their tensions." I am sure that if Mellie became the surgical nurse, she is first-rate.

Tutoring

By the third day of the nor' easter, it began to get to me. Outside, I was afraid of skidding and breaking my bones; inside, I could not see out of any of the windows and felt drugged. Cabin fever! I longed to get out and go to New York, where I imagined I would bask in the service of my little hotel, go to plays, and eat some excellent food at Madame Auxphelle's. My nose was all dried up from the radiators, which made my back warm while my feet were cold. When Mrs. Perley arrived that morning (God knows how), she said she could not have opened her door if her son had not come over to dig her out. A stealthy numbness had crept into my spirit. I stood at the window, hypnotized by the separate, innocent-looking tiny flakes as they settled on the miniature mountain outside my cave of a room. The lower part of the window was swathed in drapes of white and dappled with frost leaves.

Kate, our pre-med from Maine, came to me holding a batch of pages. "I want to know what a fictional situation is. I have to write a story and I have to use a character I have written about before, and a description I have written before."

Bravo for Mr. Taylor, I thought. "Who is the character?"

"Well, there are really two—two women, one is a drunk and one is a social worker."

"Does the description go with them?"

"Yes, but I don't know what a fictional situation *is*."

"Something has to happen to make a story, and they have to have a conflict or a problem and it has to get settled some way or other. Like this: One day I was walking along in New York, down by New York University, and I saw a boy slamming his girl into a brick wall, and she was crying, so I told him to stop it. Then he turned and spit on me, and his saliva ran down my coat. That is a fictional situation, but there isn't any story because we don't know what was going on, or why he spit on me, or how they settled their fight."

She nodded her head, looking very intent.

"So you have to make up the rest. What happened?"

Kate got up and walked out. "Goodbye, Muggs," I called after her.

Kate had grown. She was still tall, gangling, and brunette, but her hair was cut and curly now, and she smiled often. She still had the succinct approach of a New Englander who had spent her life down by the roaring Atlantic—a real Yankee. I could scarcely remember how sullen she was when we began last September. Everyone loved Kate, who became "Muggs," a real switch.

I felt like an eavesdropper every day as I sat in my sitting room eating lunch and looking at sea anemones of ice on the fire escape. The skiers who were due to leave on a one o'clock bus, plunked down on the settles in the hall to wrestle with their boots and exchange gossip. Meanwhile they groaned, "Why did I ever take up this ghastly sport?" Two or three hours later they came clumping in and flung their boots on the floor in showers of snow. "I didn't fall down once."

When the snow stopped and the sun came in, the sun, the sun! skiing was at its finest. I could hear the "plop, plop" of icicles dripping; now and then one fell with a crash.

Stamping boots, snapping buckles.

"Hey, we're going to have to *do* something about our class."

154

"Who've you got?"

"Miss Reid."

"I have Miss Larsen. I *love* Miss Larsen." Pounding and blowing.

"Lars makes fun of people who can't ski, like me."

"Damn these buckles."

"Is anybody going to the store this afternoon?"

Someone came in groaning, with great, inhaled gasps. Probably she had a letter from the boy friend.

Lisa talked through her nose. "Well, *mine* I have to write observations on—five of them. That's a hell of a lot."

"*Beardsley, come on!!!*"

"Now stick it in your ear."

"Oh, by God, I'm gonna be late."

"*Hey, Peanuts!!!*"

"I lost my ski pants."

"They're in your room."

"They are *not*."

(They lost all kinds of pants. They lost sweaters, gloves, boots, caps. Their bodies resented clothes.)

"Oh, he's married."

Lisa howled, "I *can't* wait for dinner."

(But we had just had lunch, it seemed to me.)

"What are we having?"

I couldn't hear, but I hoped it was not rubbery hamburgers.

"Well, hot shit."

"Guess what I got on my psych quiz?"

"98."

"F."

Virgie's voice, as she stamped into her boots. "This is the whole bag." She was now an Isolde with a crinkled mouth.

Someone answered. "I'm real thrilled about the whole deal, I can't wait for this skiing class to come all day." The tone was sarcastic.

"All day! All *week*."

Lisa, feeling silly, showed me later what happens when you drive your ski pole into the snow, thinking it is packed, and find it is soft. She reeled around in the middle of the hall, driving the

155

imaginary pole down, down, down, until she was tilted at an impossible angle to the floor. Her posture reminded me of what happened now when I tried to go down some steps into my basement studio. One leg went down, down, down—there was no step there.

Chace, who missed Britt, came in, stamping harder than anyone else, and singing, "You are alive, so come on out and show it!" She whooped up the stairs, "They're all out of brownies."

"Yes-o, keen-o, shit-o."

Chace, in her pale blue ski jacket with the hood tied around her face, and her long tights with ragged shorts *over* them, looked precisely like a wicked baby.

"He said they were vulgar humbugs. Chace and I thought that was cool. 'Vulgar humbugs!' We both wrote it down." They wrote down everything that was "really good." They were so alive that the past struck them as dead, but they knew when it wasn't. Every teacher who has ever collected class notes has had a shock.

I still did not know some of the girls at all, beyond their names, and Merrivale was one of them; she studied all the time and spent her evenings in the library.

One evening Merrivale came in looking morose in her long nightgown figured in green and blue, and with a wet towel over her masses of black, wet hair. Her brown eyes looked somewhat damp also; she always had a drenched appearance.

"Who is John Stuart Mill? I have to read a whole book by him, *On Liberty*, and I took an hour and a half to read fourteen pages."

I groaned. I had never read John Stuart Mill and never expected to. The English department must have had *some* reason for this assignment. But Merrivale found his nineteenth century prose tortuous and she did not have a philosophic mind. She was a memorizer of facts.

"What do you think he is noted for?"

"Utilitarianism." She pronounced this word as if it were ugly, and it is.

156

I was amused. I had thought the great man was against utilitarianism, but I was not sure. In any case, utilitarianism had reached its zenith in the United States of America. I looked it up. It proposed that a thing is worth whatever it is in terms of utility, and it was a doctrine that advocated aiming for the greatest happiness of the greatest number of people. I supposed from the TV ads that the greatest happiness of the greatest number of people depended upon the GNP; upon using ten kinds of soap, perspiration deodorants, cars, perfumes, and lawn mowers, stomach remedies, TV sets, razors, electric gadgets. Still, to be fair, perhaps this doctrine was conceived to protest against poverty and hunger, which we still have to shame us; and John Stuart Mill *did* believe in quality as well as quantity.

After we untangled a couple of nineteenth century sentences, I said, "You have to translate English into English." Merrivale looked a bit drier. Perhaps she was learning reading stamina, a branch of athletics less popular than tennis.

I tried to encourage her by reciting what she could easily have discovered in the library—"He was a very human guy. He waited for twenty years to marry the woman he loved—after her first husband died. And he dedicated 'The Essay on Liberty' to her, because she worked with him on it. Think about Women's Lib in 1859!"

She took the towel off, and shook down her long black hair. In her bright colors, she appeared to be a Hawaiian maiden. John Stuart Mill indeed!

At least there is one reason for sending girls to college; they have to discuss something besides boys, clothes, their hair, their parents, and whatever Establishment they happen to be against, in terms more complicated than "It turns me on," or "It turns me off." One Dartmouth boy said here in our midst that he would prefer an uneducated woman, and I understood his point of view—some men through the ages have liked to think of woman as a chattel. But my own experience has taught me that a reasonable number of men are more intelligent that I am and are looking for a woman who will not bore them to death. A woman

157

can give her body to a stupid man or a brilliant one, but he will not get the whole woman unless he is at least as intelligent as she is.

The English department had hit upon an interesting assignment. They wanted to know why the girls like Rod McKuen. I was dismayed to be consulted, for I knew nothing of Rod McKuen, who wrote what the girls called poetry, combined with a musical setting.

"You should listen to 'The Sea,'" they said. "It has a lot of seagulls and everything."

Lisa came in and said she wanted to compare Rod McKuen to T.S. Eliot and Dylan Thomas. This seemed a trifle ambitious to complete by the next day.

Finally a group came in and settled on the floor.

"You are all sentimentalists," I said.

"That's right," a chorus answered.

"Why do you pretend to be hard and tough?"

No one knew. Everyone drew into her shell like a turtle. Lisa said, "I only get D's on papers, no matter what I do!"

"When I was young, we liked 'Blue Skies,' and 'Always,' and 'Remember,' and we danced with our arms around boys' necks and wore long, filmy dresses and taffeta ruffles. We were sentimentalists and everyone knew it. We believed in romance and America and houses with ruffled curtains."

"We do all that, too, when we are up in Hanover, in fraternity houses."

This was at variance with a tale I heard about how the Theta Delts had terrific food fights and one girl got a bloody nose from being hit by a chicken bone. I didn't remember anything like that from my weekends at the Beta house at the University of Michigan, circa 1928. But I did remember sitting on my fiance's lap all night in a big red leather chair in a room where no one ever turned on the lights.

We began reading bad lines from Rod and good lines from Rod. I suspected that the English department was out to prove that only a genius of a writer could stand a rigorous criticism.

"Well, everyone has escapes," I said. "I like English detective stories and some of your fathers like westerns and perhaps your mothers like weepy movies about misunderstood ladies."

158

I really did a cop-out on that one.

I didn't envy the English department their job with Rod McKuen and the seagulls. But I wished the girls would ask them what *their* escapes were, and insist on a truthful answer.

Maria came in with an excellent poem called "Shadow Silhouettes," about being in bed with her brown skin on white sheets. It was total integration.

"Was he a black guy or a white guy?"

"He was a white guy and he invited his 'hometown honey' to the Winter Carnival, the bastard."

I was so impressed by Maria's freedom of speech that for a moment I regretted the repressive good taste of my generation, the silence about love affairs all the more delightful for being kept private.

But I was convinced that the generations were not so different as most imagined. The trouble was that the older generation was too cowardly to tell the younger ones what *we* did. And maybe the English department had not explained about Doll Tearsheet in Shakespeare, or "The Miller's Tale" in Chaucer.

We had, officially, nineteen inches of snow piled on top of God-knows-how-many; we now walked between banks seven or eight feet high.

Mr. Rufus and I were making up.

"Do you want me to move my car so you can plow?"

"If you want to." Mr. Rufus was a rugged disciplinarian. Far be it from him to tell me what to do if I had not sense enough to get the message after I spent four dollars to get the car dug out last time.

One morning I woke up and decided that I had an empty, anesthetized place in my head caused by silly conversation, hibernation, and *girls*. The solution to this was outrageously presumptuous, but it worked. I got in my car and drove to Hanover, parked the car, and walked up three flights of stairs to the English office in Sanborn Hall. A lovely, bookish smell, leather, old wood, print, confusion, papers, home.

"I want to see Richard Eberhart." I was trembling. I waited for an hour, then the door opened, and a round head peered out. A ruddy face, a gentle air, a slightly crooked mouth.

"Come in." The office was old, shabby, unpretentious, warm with the teaching of a lifetime. The stunning impact of his poem, "The Fury of Aerial Bombardment" rang in my head. Richard Eberhart smiled. It was a sunny smile.

I said, "I have to *hear* some poetry." I tried to explain.

"Well," he said, folding his hands on his chest above his stomach, "I will be having a class of ten boys and one girl who write poetry, at my house one evening a week. The college doesn't permit auditing, but you may come as a guest." I was speechless with gratitude.

"Just check the catalogue for the spring term," he said. So it was that all through the spring I drove to Hanover one evening a week to the home of Richard and Betty Eberhart, where ten boys, one girl, and I were together. When a poem was particularly bad, Professor Eberhart would smile beneficently and say, "It could have been a lot worse."

So much has been written about Richard Eberhart as a poet; we did not hear his poetry. The boys read *their* poetry, and the girl read *her* poetry. Betty gave us doughnuts and hot cider, and we listened to teaching so effortless, unplanned, spontaneous, that it was a fire in the mind.

Valentine's Day

Vicki knocked on my door and shyly handed in a florist's box she had found on the front stoop. "These are for you." Vicki was so loving and quiet that one always felt like saying, "Bless you." Her voice, her face spoke of what we called good breeding.

There were a dozen beautiful fragrant red roses. I put them in a tall transparent glass vase on the harvest table in the hall, where they were reflected in a large mirror.

At first, the girls saw only the box in the hall wastebasket. "Who got flowers?"

They sounded a bit dashed when they found out it was I who got the roses. They did not like "old people" to seem young, and I couldn't explain about the roses or old love. It is difficult for my generation to seem old, for we spent our youth trying to please our parents, and our middle age trying to please our children, frequently blowing up from frustration. Now that we are contemplating old age, we have not found our own style; besides, "being old" is a dirty phrase in this country and one is reproved for using it.

Legs moaned, pulling at her jacket sleeves, "I'll bet I don't even get a Valentine card—Jack will forget. Maybe my father —" her father was evidently to be counted upon. Several other girls looked silently envious.

"Oh, *roses!*" They smelled them. Roses in the snow.

Maria said, "Oh, beautiful flowers." She was wearing a big flowered hat with a brim. She began to sing down the hall, "I wish Danny would send me some flowers, I wish Danny would send me some flowers." She was making up the music. Was Danny the "bastard" I heard of so recently? Maria's moods rose and fell like rockets on Independence Day.

I went across to my room and sank into the old brown easy chair. The gossamer fantasies of the girls seemed so fragile, so easily torn. Memories! I had too many. One could not sort out all the memories, the wrong turnings, the right moments, the cost. And I felt the texture of reality as I knew it; the thick, resilient, woven material that stretched and grew threadbare but sufficed to clothe my vulnerable self. For the red roses were, in an unconscious way, a forcible entry, like the old love who sent them, an embarrassment, a reminder thrust into old wounds. Sentimentality and cruelty—two sides of a coin tossed up for winning or losing, as if love were a contest. Is it a misfortune to love always everybody one has ever loved? But in a different *way* when passion is dead . . . Faulkner's "A Rose For Emily" makes me shudder . . . necrophilia. What is fidelity? To me, something beyond gestures, a faithfulness beyond the bed, one's own private truth which surfaces after passion (or a dutiful accommodation), a commanding fulfillment or revulsion. Fidelity is not an act of will—it happens, and when it does not happen, choices remain; one choice is to be faithful to oneself, the private self.

Somber thoughts. It was too far to go back. The old keep their secrets because, as Thornton Wilder said, "Everyone has a right to make his own mistakes," and I have relished some of mine. The roses evoked a humorous memory of the time I received a purple orchid one evening when I was wearing a tweed topcoat and a head scarf! There is something to be said for having lived, as Hermione Gingold made clear in "A Little

162

Night Music," sitting in her wheel chair and reciting with gusto to her granddaughter the joys of her distinguished purple past uncluttered by guilt.

Almost time for dinner. When I went out, Rae came in, wearing her famous fake furry coat and a real fur bonnet, a real live Teddy bear with pink cheeks. "I wish Desmond would send *me* roses."

"Some day someone will."

She rolled her eyes like a yearning cocker spaniel.

"No. Lots of my friends have had roses, and I *never* have."

Obviously I had been gauche.

"Who got the flowers?" Small moans.

I began to see that they loved roses as a symbol of romance; *who* got them seemed to be more important than the fact that they were here, glowing and deliciously fragrant, multiplying themselves in the mirror.

Merrivale squealed. "Oh, aren't those *neat!* Oh, aren't roses *wonderful!*" Her eyes were sparkling.

I began to feel as if I should not have placed the roses in the public domain. "It isn't fair for me to have them, is it? Should I hide them?"

Pat was generous as always. "No, leave them out where we can all see them and smell them—I think it's great." Pat had a package and a Valentine card from her father, who didn't mind admitting that she was his little sweetheart.

Virgie, who was quiet these days, beamed with a soft, radiant look. Could this be the Virgie who arrived so explosively in September?

I had a strange fantasy, and I wished I were in the movie business, so I could show it. What if we all got some red roses? The roof would be wafted off the house, and the walls would fall out into the snow without a sound, slowly, slowly, and in all the rooms girls would be swooning like dying swans. Roses could change their world, at least if they never went outside.

SPRING

Solitude Enjoyed

Something had happened to me since Christmas when I had rushed out of Bixby dorm as if pursued by the furies of loneliness; I was spending spring vacation in the dorm alone. I did not fear the isolation; the emptiness was gone, and in its place was a feeling I had as a child but lost—perhaps the first time I looked in the mirror and saw the signs of age in my own face. Now I had a sensation of enjoyment. A long conversation with myself was coming into focus.

When the girls departed in their usual flurry of screams and luggage and parents and boy friends, I was glad to see them go. I was now the sole occupant of an enormous estate; at night there were few lights except the one shining in my room, the lights in the bell tower, or the gentle tall lantern lights that stood around the quad. The whole campus was still snowy, and on sunny mornings I awoke to absolute quiet and got up to look out at the acres of peace.

Mary Barnes told me that I really should "inspect" the girls' rooms during the holiday; this was something I had never done before. I had a conviction they should live as they pleased inside their own rooms, as long as they were not damaging the property.

The long corridors stretched silently before my feet; third floor, second floor, first floor, and I looked into various nests which seemed designed for agoraphobia. There were the ubiquitous animals, small and cozy, or great, plushy, and stiff, living on the beds, in corners, or on chairs covered with vivid cotton prints. There were tiny bottles of cosmetics and scent in great disarray on dressers, and curtains of colored beads. It was all a jumble, with no thought of a combination into a coherent design, containing open spaces.

The rugs wrinkled and squirmed from running feet; the armchairs writhed from living bodies sitting in them, hanging legs over arms, or pummeling into them from an excess of fury at books. Books! They were everywhere, as perhaps they never would be again, books that were really used, dug into, underlined, and almost torn from their covers. In the future, perhaps books would be kept on shelves or neatly stacked on coffee tables. These books look *lived* with. Bedspreads were batik prints, or pastel cotton candlewicks, all of them thrown over rumpled blankets until the beds looked like overstuffed fat ladies whose dresses didn't quite fit.

I saw snapshots of friends stuck in mirror frames; the big photographs of boy friends and mother and fathers were gone from the scene.

I looked into the room of orderly Vicki and small, dignified Peanuts, and the jumble resolved into blue and white order, a feeling of balance. Vicki's collages hung on the walls, and they reflected Vicki's temperament, a serenity not yet exploded by violent emotion. Vicki and Peanuts were tidy, warm people.

When I came to Ginevra's room, I hesitated. The memory of searching it on that terrible night when we learned to know Becky was still with me. But finally I opened the door. For a long time last fall a sign hung on the door saying no one was to come in without permission, but now this was gone and in place of it there was a poster saying "Dragon Ay" in red, with a mystical design below that. The tall windows had no curtains or shades, and the light flooded in. Hanging from strings in one window were Oriental wind chimes of brass; I went in and touched them gently and they gave a silvery sound. Beside this window the Chicago Seven stared from a large poster, posed in a gloomy chiaroscuro, looking as formal as an old daguerreotype. Under this serious picture, an April calendar with Joan Anglund children catching butterflies made a sentimental note in pale blue, yellow, and green.

I saw again the large candles on the windowsill, red, lavender, and orange, and a small green vase with a spray of dried purple flowers, and I remembered how Ginevra burned the candles in the evening and played her stereo: fire and music and the smell of incense. Becky's bed had been removed except for the mattress and springs, which were now a low couch on the floor covered with a spread from India and a red blanket across the foot. Ginevra's bed was made up neatly with a Madras spread of green, purple and blue.

Only one thing spoke of childhood: on the dresser which was covered by a long fringed cerise shawl a little Pocket Doll stood dressed in a white cap and apron over a pink dress, and at her feet there was a yellow fuzzy chicken with big orange felt feet, looking squashed and silly.

I looked at the Indian portrait, *Cannabis Rex;* he was covered with medals, and wore a feather in his hat, a heart medallion around his neck. He was smoking an enormous cigar. And I looked at a fine ink drawing of a naked couple embracing, their bodies in "negative space." There were two serene landscapes also. Then I went out and closed the door. Ginevra had a sense of atmosphere. This was her room and it could not belong to anyone else.

And finally, I went down to the Butt. It was uncommonly neat, owing to the efforts of Mrs. Perley, but as green and dreary as ever, as if it were some cavern in a sluggish sea. On a table I found the remains of someone's struggle with a paper on Soviet youth, and a little red notebook. The girls were always beginning little notebooks to remind them of assignments, but the notebooks were so small that they were soon lost, for who carried purses except on journeys out into the world? And the notebooks fell from pockets to join the trail of lost objects left everywhere.

In the little notebook only three pages were filled, for the notes had begun in someone's fine resolution to become more tidy and efficient, but all this had been abandoned. The notebook began like this: "Wed. homework—English—author reports. Begin to take notes on progress of question. Bought books! Spanish—conversation; chaps 17 and voc. (all) test. Algebra—pg. 279 (1-32) U.S. Hist. Read pgs. 501-503. Human Rel. make-ups! Exercise pg. 10 (matching); Chapter 1 pg. 9 (3,4,5) Chap. 2—may substitute (2,3,5). Summary on phil. pamphlet. Chap. 7 Notes, Read Chap. 8. Read Chaps. 9, 10, 11."

After this the notes gave up, and no wonder. I was exhausted merely from reading them. The notebook then decided to keep up its spirits by looking to the future. "Ranch date notes—trip March 6, 7, 8 Boston kids. Campers—Aug. 2 - 9. Work crew dates—July 16 - Aug. 9 - Sept. 6. Chris calling Sat. afternoon. Put ticket in wallet! Call Mom."

Here the notebook gave up completely on the world, present or future, and a poem appeared, carefully printed.

> I look to the wall for an answer
> But nothing bounces off the concrete
> Just a whirl of nothingness
> That doesn't penetrate my ears.
>
> I look to my parents for an answer
> But my mouth freezes my thoughts
> And my mind fizzles
> And I stand . . . alone.
> I look to my friends for an answer
> Meaningless words fill the room
> The question unsolved
> The friends . . . and I stand alone
>
> So now I turn to my God
> And he whispers the answer, I love,
> He said, and I come to you
> To make you his

170

I am happy now
For I have Him
He has me
And I had you.

After some scribbling I couldn't read, it said, "Stacy owes me $1.00."

I climbed back upstairs. The girls would be back soon, and it seemed to me the house had begun to lose its untenanted smell and its unlived-in look. I was ready for the girls to come back, but something new had happened; I was ready to live without them. I felt no fear here alone. Some chemistry of the spirit had brought me to the time of liking to be where I was.

I read during this time that the great psychoanalyst, Erikson, had named my time of life one of "integrity or despair." But neither of these quite fitted. I did not always look back with complete integrity; neither did I feel despair.

What! A great blowing snowstorm was beginning over the feathery, budding trees; the wind was whining in fury. I looked at the pot of daffodils I had purchased only a few days before. Could this be *April 1?* The snowplow was creaking, rattling, and jerking like an old dinosaur ready to give a few gasps before extinction. I decided it would be fun to blow along to the Inn and have some drinks and a very good dinner. The dark held no terrors, and I was hungry for food created in a Real Kitchen. As I donned my layers of warmth, pulled on my boots, I thought of two martinis at the little bar presided over by Mr. Littlehale, the innkeeper, and a chat with Mrs. Littlehale by the fire in the lounge—and then—beef stroganoff? or Cornish hen with orange sauce? a crunchy salad, some home-baked pie, excellent coffee. I felt I would be among friends and if the storm increased, someone would see me home.

Love, War, Death, and Poetry

After the spring holiday, everyone returned full of *zing*.
Beatrice, dressed in red, white and blue striped pants and a navy
sweater, with white Dutch clogs on her feet, got to work at once
making the bulletin board proclaim a new season. Down came
all the tired winter notices; up went a background of lemon
yellow, with paper flowers in pastels blooming at every corner.
    She had been to Florida. "That's a great tan you have," I
said. She was more of a nut-brown maiden than ever.
    "It's all fading," she said wistfully, looking back over her
shoulder as she pushed in thumbtacks.
    Rae came swooping through the hall dressed like a lady
who is either going to a ball or her boudoir, I couldn't decide
which. She floated in her long filmy gown printed in pale blues,
yellows, and pinks, with wing-like sleeves and a low neck
surrounded by rhinestones; on her feet she had exotic sandals
with more glittering stones. Her hair was swinging around her
face.
    She raised her arms, and the sleeves floated out.
    "You are looking quite glamorous."

172

"Well, I was so sure that I'd be invited to the Green Key at Dartmouth that I got ready."

A short time later I saw her looking childish in a short nightgown.

Barbie rushed in and did a jig with me. She had been accepted in the lab at Stanford University Hospital. She dangled silver bracelets and earrings and pins before my eyes. "I've learned how to make silver jewelry! It's so much fun, and oh, the money it brings in! I spent forty dollars on silver and stuff!" Why was Barbie a pre-med?

I went to sleep hearing someone struggling in with her suitcases from the late bus, saying, "My arms are pulling out of their sockets." Then suitcases bumped on the stairs, and someone else said, "Shhhhhh."

The next morning when I saw three small figures trudging out to class in their old blue jeans and navy jackets and sloppy shirts, I realized they dressed like laborers when it was time to labor, but one of these was Les, who turned off to the infirmary with her lips all sore from an infection, yelling, "I can't *kiss* anybody!" as if this were really the worst thing in the world.

The weather became divinely warm and full of promise. The girls took this as a signal to pursue their favorite sport, consorting with the other sex. Libido was exploding faster than the leaves that had begun to turn the trees and shrubs a pinkish and tender color; the willows were quickening with pale yellow hair, the birches topped by delicate blackish lace. The snow had melted until we could see little rivulets on the walks, and we could foresee where the grass would grow out of the mud. Mrs. Perley was mopping up muddy tracks on all the carpets.

Barbie said the dentist had given her too much gas during vacation, and now she knew why people go mad; she dreamed, while awake, and with her body numb, that she fell into a great void and the world ended, and she was the only one left, "Like the last little period," she said, "like in an oatmeal box, and I was a tiny, infinitesimal little thing who had to do something, but if the world ended, God was ended, and I had nothing left." She shook as she told me this. "And last night when I went to sleep, I dreamed it again."

I stared at Barbie. Could it be that this rosy, jolly, outward person could have such a fear deep in her psyche? If so, it was proof, yes, this was proof, that even the healthiest person is afraid of an ultimate nothingness.

"Could be you have had enough responsibility for awhile," I said. I knew exactly what she was talking about, but I didn't want to admit it to Barbie, who was ordinarily as introspective as a daffodil.

Boys were sprouting up faster than hyacinths. They came in and out of the house all day now; some of them were long and lanky, with light hair and glasses, and some came charging in by threes, husky and blue-jeaned, demanding to see Maria, who came out in a dark blue robe over some flowered panties and a pink bra, her body showing as she walked, as slender as an exquisite brown lily.

"What have you got on under that robe?" the horniest and biggest boy asked, and for an answer, Maria flicked her robe aside in a maddening gesture with a wicked smile to match. Then she went to the piano and began singing, and they all sat entirely hypnotized.

"We have oodles of girls," Maria said the them. I wondered what in the devil Maria thought this was, a brothel? But I was mildly envious because she knew What It Is All About.

Other boys roared up in sports cars and rolled in like tumbleweeds. Merton left on our hall table an immense poster photograph of himself with Fannie, a girl I didn't know very well, both of them looking so wacky that they must have been on a "trip" when it was taken. The picture made me feel that if there was anything more sweetly and stickily sentimental than a group of old ladies at a baby shower, it was some of our dear young potheads on a trip and exuding a hopped-up love.

Bright spring. "I just got a phone call from a boy. Ricky. He's my daily lover. He checks up on me twenty-four hours a day," came a voice from the hall.

I began to think of summer, of green leaves swaying on a hot day, of swimming in a lake, of running through deep grass, of sweat dripping down from too much sun, of tennis and ice cream cones.

Somewhere in the far reaches of the upstairs corridors a girl was singing raucously, "Look inside, girl! I'm in love, love, love, I'm in love, love, love!"

"Knock if off, will you? a calmer voice demanded.

The answer to this was a prolonged screaming, a tearing out of a throat.

The screaming voice yelled, "Yoo-hooooooooooooo," and "Love, love, love!" It was a vocal, throaty orgasm.

Feet pounded upstairs, and there were a few remote, subsiding moans.

Not all of love was cheerful; is it ever? Spring is a free-wheeling time of wildness, with passion and disappointment sometimes sharper, as if the heart and guts have been opened to all feeling and expression by the rebirth of all growing things. In the spring I came to know Brandie, the owl-eyed, twiggy girl. Her reactions to spring were composed of the discovery of poetry and the alleviation of her loneliness for a boy friend in San Francisco by going out with a wild-eyed young man namned Preston, who had been in Vietnam for twenty-three months and was going back. Preston was nervous and covered it with callousness; he never stopped talking in a loud voice. He had bitter blue eyes and blonde hair cropped so short that he looked almost bald, so he wore a little brimmed straw hat with a plaid band in the house and out. His idea of humor was to ask me if I had a date. I felt that Preston had settled for Vietnam until he had almost gone mad, but he came and sat around in our living room as if he found it soothing. Brandie said she "had a gas" with him one Friday night. Somehow Brandie, with her big glasses and thin, small body and quick movements, had in her a mysterious quality of passion and fun in a mixture that burned up without smoke, like a good French farce.

One evening, I heard piercing yells, and walked around the corner to observe Brandie's Vietnam veteran wrestling with her in the hall; he had her in an elbow lock, and she was struggling with a will. Brandie was laughing. "O, *stop* it, Preston, you're *hurting* me!" I felt terror as I saw his face, contorted by violence, his teeth gritting—all the killing he had seen, all the love he could not find, the fury of his despair at "having fun" when he needed passion that went deep and healing into his frightened body. I ran to him. "Preston, *please*." Had Brandie teased and baited him with her wit, her gayety, her deep-down romantic love for someone far away? Or, and I felt my anger rising, with her hands? She was still laughing and struggling like a child, and Preston's face, as he looked up, mirrored murder. I put my hand firmly on the arm which held Brandie, then on the hand which could snap her little bones. "Preston." And he let go, but he wept. Brandie turned white with fear. "He hit me." She went upstairs.

Through all this hurly-burly, the little straw hat stayed on. Now he took it off and followed me into the living room where I sat down, stunned by what these girls did not know of sex and aggression; of how, in an instant, passion can turn to anger, to the ferocity of fire contained or unloosed, sometimes exciting, sometimes dangerous.

But one I knew of was wise beyond her age, the quietest girl in the dorm; she had told me of taking a taxi on the final lap of her return from the spring holiday, and the old driver had turned into a dark side road to force her into sex.

"What did you do?"

"I talked him out of it." Still shaking, she told me this with inner composure. "I was so *frightened*." I could not speak then, wondering at this shy girl who had all this strength, the man who responded, who finally brought her to the dorm unharmed. Then I said, "You were lucky."

Preston stood there before me, nervous, shaken; he had a tender respect hard to fathom, as if far back in his boyhood he had learned what the bloody callousness of Vietnam had not stripped from him. And I heard him apologizing for *rudeness!* "I'm really sorry, ma'am, please forgive me." Not a word about Brandie. He shook my hand three times, then he bent and kissed my cheek twice. I could feel a choking in my throat, a puckering of my mouth, as I tried to keep from letting a sob come out.

"Please sit down, Preston." He sat, twitching, and put his hat on his shaved head. "The girls don't understand. They have

176

sex in the head and Vietnam on TV." His bitter blue eyes glared. "How old are you?"

"Twenty-four."

"How long have you been in the Army?"

"Six years."

"Must you go back to Vietnam after twenty-three months?"

"I have to . . . " In his face I saw madness; he had given up whatever life was. "I am going tomorrow." There was nothing I could do for this wild, ruined boy. But for a few minutes, we sat there for the only time I ever saw Preston quiet. I was thirty-three and divorced in 1941, and I was remembering sitting up all night with a big, gentle Army officer named Jack who was going with Patton's Army to Africa. "I'm so scared," he said. "Please just stay with me." And there were all those V-mail letters, and falling in love three times with men who did not come back. They did not feel dishonored in that war. Those were parlous times for women then, for along with the frantic pace, we learned (and could recite) the Article of War which court-martialed a man for rape. We learned not to tease a desperate and determined man; and we learned that a man can be impotent because he is so lonely for his own wife. One of these lay all night beside me on the grass by a swimming pool, and tenderly kissed me and smoothed my hair while he told me about his one true love. At dawn he said, "Thank you," and left as all of them did, frightened of mutilation or death.

I was furiously angry with Brandie, but to no purpose. Girls were coming and going as if nothing very remarkable had happened; Preston was "a nut," and Brandie liked tussling, liked fun with a dash of bitters. I rose, and Preston stood quickly, like a well-trained little boy who jumped to his feet with the carnage, the blood, the groans of burning bodies, the explosions in his ears all about us in this cool green room. Broken, hopelessly split. His eyes turned appealing as he said "Goodbye," almost jauntily, while his face resumed the mask, hard as granite, furrowed with bewildered cynicism, coarsened by hysterical glee. When he left, Rae, who was typing a paper on the Hindu religion, came out, shook her head, and remarked, "That boy just can't stop. He will go on until he cracks up." We

177

were all due to crack up over Vietnam, and it would leave us with a legacy of pity and shame, of humiliation; refugees, orphans, young men disabled, drugs, a futile war.

I came to know Carol in spring, for Carol's father had a malignant brain tumor and the prognosis was that he had two months to live. Carol was a *plus* person who countered minuses with more pluses and a love of life. Even with a sword hanging over her head, she could come in yelling and dancing because "It's so *great* outdoors!"

The somber notes of spring: the War, death, the imminent farewells—the immense dark cloud of Cambodia, of Kent State approaching, as we lived in our sunlit world after the pinched cold of the long winter—Victoria, returned from New York; she had seen Harlem now.

I was seeing the boys differently at Richard Eberhart's in Hanover where they lay on the floor and read their poetry; about this they were quite serious. Professor Eberhart sat in an old red leather chair, worn to the shape of his round body, blackened in spots until it was like an old leather shoe, his beautiful long hands folded on his chest—a ruddy face, a gentle air, a fatherly tone when the slightly crooked mouth said, "You boys are the creative life here." The poetry was somber, bitter . . . " the disemboweled body of a twelve-year-old girl by a roadside near Phum Vieng Duong . . . "Soon our children's children's children/Dressed in black bark, will be chewing cats and dogs." But the hunger for love blossomed there also, naked and unashamed, "You were violets" . . . "Girl, I'd rather run my fingers over your bod/ than go shake hands with old Mr. God." . . . "The face that smiles/ It's the seeing/ It's the hearing/ It's the touching/ And knowing./ I love you in the morning."

The violence and need of Preston became explicit in these spring evenings of the young male voices reading, and in the answering voice of the one girl in the class, "yet a muted wind/ whistles scenes/of blood and killing/in my mind," or her mem-

178

ories of "Ernie and his 1953 custom straight eight" . . . "we grew that summer—/like creeping rust or the/shredding seams in the canvas roof/that let us glimpse the stars at dawn . . . i dreamed i saw that car again—/mired in a daisy field/and choked with broken glass and rust:/reflections of the past and now:/the future folded in a map."

Love and Death, the agenda for Spring, 1970. Subjects too profound for anyone to experience casually in everyday life. They coped with these by the same means we all use, work, play, humor, love for *someone*. I had not gone to college in wartime, but rather in 1926-1930. Richard Eberhart remembered. "The Fury of Aerial Bombardment" was written out of anger and compassion. I went back from this class every week awed by his gentleness with the boys, his firm recognition. I came back to the dorm each time wanting to be more patient, more aware of how what seemed foolish to me was a healthy defense to break the tensions of worry; the conflict between wanting to go out into the uncertain world and the longing to stay a child on a well-known merry-go-round.

One evening we had a session on modern poetry, inspired by Brandie, who said she couldn't understand the poems. We were joined by Tuttle and Maria; the girls sprawled on the floor as was their wont, and I sat in a chair because my skirt was too tight for me to get down with them. (This was perhaps symbolic.) Brandie looked wise in her big horn-rimmed glasses, as if she could understand anything in the world, and she had stopped moaning about how she wouldn't graduate. Tuttle lay on her side looking comfortable in her ragged jeans, and Maria looked plain beautiful.

I had begun to feel vaguely nostalgic over the ending of the year, the anticipation of goodbyes, my own graduation. We had decided on William Carlos Williams for the entree and never got any further after one hour and a half.

"I'm beginning to dig this guy," Brandie said as a preamble. "I got 70 today in a quiz on this in class."

"He writes about commonplace things in life—he was a

doctor, and delivered babies, and he saw that all life is part of one thing."

We read "Rain," and heard the rain down-dripping over everything. "He says it is like a woman's love," I suggested.

They nodded. "You have to swing with it, the way you rock to rock music—every poem has its own rhythm. You have to get with it," I said.

We got with it. We read "The Yachts" and played the record where Dr. Williams read the poem in a dry, trembling old voice. "Who are these dead hands and faces of agony clutching at the beautiful yachts?"

"I think they are the waves," Maria said. I did not argue.

We read about the barren weeds of early spring and the quickening into life, and we read "Tract" about how to have a funeral without a black, shiny hearse and glass windows, and without hothouse flowers. Me: "Who is talking about the funeral?"

"The dead," Brandie said, and we talked about Martin Luther King and his plain wooden cart.

People came in and interrupted. "You have a long distance call, Tuttle." She ran out, but we went on reading, and she got back in a few minutes. My sitting room felt warm and close, cosy with learning together. What I don't know about William Carlos Williams is volumes.

A poem is like a fan one must open to see the design, and the poems opened of themselves, spreading before us their revealing images; and the girls opened as the poems opened. Their faces lost all look of worry and discontent and became questions of wonder.

We had a hard time with "These."

"Well, it's doom and gloom, like falling into the void. Did you ever feel as if you had fallen into space and there was nothing there, and you couldn't fall or get back—at the dentist's—remember?" I was thinking of Barbie.

Everyone looked comprehending. No one spoke.

"But the 'source of poetry' turns the stone, the hard, unyielding despair, into the flashing waters."

Heads nodded. But after awhile, they were tired. It was

taxing to be young and to explore the mind of an old man as complex as Williams. We ended with playing the speech of Dylan Thomas on "A Visit to America," where he etched in glittering wit the experience of a poet in the boondocks of the culture vultures. Tuttle laughed so hard that she cried. I wanted them to know that a great poet can be funnier than the joke boys on TV.

Barbie came in and chewed on a chocolate-covered graham cracker and drank several mugs of Hawaiian punch. Barbie did not "dig" poetry. She was basking in the relief from doing all the onerous tasks and joyous about unloading them on Beatrice, the vice-president of the house.

"I'm giving Balls all the little, diddly things to do, like checking when the girls get in at night. Whew! It's great. Last night I came in and I knew I was going to cry, so I cried for thirty minutes. It was funny seeing Tuttle while I cried and wailed— my turn."

When I went to my room I thought, no wonder the barren weeds and the stone are foreign to them—for they *are* the spring and the flashing waters. What would they say if I told them they *are* poetry? They would say I was crazy.

The next day Brandie said, "I was *brilliant* in poetry class today! There I was, waving my hand, and I asked him a question he couldn't answer, too." From the way she said this, with an air of exultant victory, I gather that if teachers did not know the answers to questions, they would greatly enhance the student ego.

On another evening, as I walked across the front hall, I saw Junie, a very shy freshman (one who had nevertheless refused to wear her beanie) sitting on a straight chair, dressed in a long flannel pink nightgown with tiny blue flowers all over it. She was holding in her hands *The Collected Poems of Dylan Thomas*. Her round little face was bent over the book, and her brown hair was like a veil.

She looked up and said, "I saw that you have the records of Dylan Thomas, and my sister gave me this book, and I do not have a record player."

"Ah." What is there to say when someone is about to hear the voice of Dylan Thomas for the first time?

"Come on," I said. We went into the sitting room and she sat down on the floor by the record player, took the records, and carefully wrote down the page numbers of the poems she was going to hear.

I put on the record, turned the player on, and the resonant, glorious voice surged out from this man who drank himself to death, unable to contain all the life that possessed him: "Fern Hill," the green, sweet youth, "Do Not Go Gentle into That Good Night," the firm defiance of death and sorrow, "If I Were Tickled by the Rib of Love," pure sex with love from a man who held Wales in his arms and wrote "for the love of man and in praise of God. . . ."

I went out and closed the door, but across the hall, with two doors closed between us, I could hear the magnificent voice rising and falling like the sea.

At last I heard, from tones only, "After the first death, there is no other," followed by silence.

I went back and found Junie still sitting, as if she had been in another world and had not yet returned.

"Do you want to hear the other side?"

"No, not tonight." The power and the glory is not to be experienced in large doses. I stood looking at Junie sitting there in her child's nightgown in a pool of lamplight on the blue rug, and I remembered the night I heard Dylan Thomas in New York, two weeks before he died; I walked out in the rain and forgot to put my raincoat on, arriving home drenched.

Junie took her book and went upstairs as if wafted up; she walked so lightly in her soft slippers that she seemed not to feel the old, battered stairs under her feet.

At a house council meeting, Ellen had said she thought Junie was not happy. "She is so quiet."

What is happy? What is happiness? But as I learned later on, Junie's mother had leukemia. When I heard this, she had been trying for days to keep it to herself, but finally she came to me almost wordless. I could see she was suffering deeply. Dear Junie, her shoes untied, twisting her feet, hanging onto her books as if they were the only reality in the world, until I took them from her and gave her some Kleenex. Then she cried and

182

cried until she had to go to the infirmary to rest and try to absorb the news that was so shocking.

Finally I went over to see her and found her huddled in bed. "You have to let me call your father."

She turned a weary face to me. "He wants me to stay here and do my work."

"Will *you* call him?" Finally she agreed.

Before I left, she said, "Mother is a nurse and she is being wonderful. And my grandmother says it should be *her*." I have always thought of Junie as "Little Miss Muffet." As I looked at her, I remembered my first grandchild saying to me, "Why don't you put me in my room so I can cry?"

Junie went home, then she returned and carried on like a thoroughbred. Why are some people selected so young to endure the stunning confrontation with death? It is now ten years later, and I know Junie was killed in an automobile accident—when, where? I may never know.

The death of Carol's father came that spring. I gave to Carol something I had found in my mother's writing case after she died, as if she had left it there for me to find. It was a quotation from the Greek Stoic, Zeno. I remember thinking that this was strange, for my mother was a Quaker by upbringing and an old-fashioned Christian; but the message told me that before Christianity, man believed some part of the soul lived on.

> Be not afraid of death,
> For it may be a long wandering through beauty,
> Cool beauty like that of the stars,
> Warm beauty like that of the sun,
> And we will say, "What fools we were
> To dread this loveliness."

One of the odd things happening to me during this time was that I was not as afraid of death as in my youth, while becoming ever more aware of its reality. What was this—Nature? My mother, with her great sense of humor, wrote elsewhere that she would be uncomfortable in a heaven of marble mansions and golden streets—grandeur was not her style. "I won't need my false teeth, arch supports, glasses, or bum heart in heaven," she wrote. I think her idea of heaven was abstract, a new state of being somewhere in space.

Of my father, who was adamant about locking up doors, windows, valuables, and the car, she remarked, "Your father will have his crown padlocked on his head by the River Jordan."

One evening in spring, Virgie came flying out of the phone booth, bursting with a different message.

"Hey, everybody! My mother has had a baby, and it is a girl! Number six! I'm going home to see it!"

I read in the *New York Times* that Jean Stafford's *Collected Short Stories* was out; and the review by Guy Davenport contained this statement: " . . . man is a double prisoner. . . . Those who escape from the prison of family and institutions—characters who are usually independent, stubborn, or rambunctious—only to enslave themselves the more securely in the prison of self."

The girls had not escaped from family, institutions, *or* self. Was this why they were so vivid, so free? It was a paradox. They helped me to escape from the prison of self, as birds do when they light on the window of a prisoner's cell and sometimes come inside.

Chace and Tuttle

With the burgeoning of spring, I observed a few girls out in the sun with sun reflectors around their necks, catching the sun as ladies used to catch rainwater for washing their hair. Bikinis—shorts—skin, acres of it, gleaming with suntan oil.

And one Sunday, I observed Chace and Tuttle setting forth on an expedition inspired by their current study of *Huckleberry Finn*. They were dressed in pants and jackets, and Chace had a knapsack slung over her shoulder for authenticity. I wondered if Huck had a knapsack or just a "bag of vittles"? They chortled their way down the front walk, waving goodbye as if they hoped they might get lost in a cave somewhere and be found by a herd of men with flashlights.

Chace had been lonely since Britt left us and almost every day played the piano with a sound of hammers and ringing gongs, singing "Heart and Soul" as if this were a necessary ritual to staying sane until she had pounded out of herself all she could not say in words. She dreaded communication so passionately that she would not make a phone call unless her chosen mentor, Tuttle, went with her into the phone booth and put the money in for her to get the process started.

Tuttle, who always reminded me of Giulietta Massina in "La Strada," half gamine and half clown, played the piano with a tentative, exploring touch as if she were asking questions.

These two were in the very last stage of a girl's life when bumming around with another girl was more fun than going out on dates; Tuttle was merely waiting for the right man, and sometimes she got very tired of the little girl in Chace. They seemed at times like two mischievous little boys—at other times sharply divided females, and one evening at midnight I heard Tuttle out in the living room asking in a beery voice if I were around. I came out and found her sprawled in a chair. For the next hour and a half I listened while she told me that Chace was driving her crazy.

"She is so *dependent*," Tuttle wailed, sitting on the floor in her dungarees which were soaked from the melting snow in some woodsy beer garden. "I have to button her pants and help her make phone calls and wait for her everywhere we go, and if I turn her off, she will tell everyone on the dorm how mean I am."

I was astounded. I had supposed Tuttle and Chace were bosom friends who liked to share everything; now I realized that Tuttle had outgrown this. Also I wondered if I were not hearing the story of many emotional attachments; one of the two drains the other dry. Tuttle pulled her hair, stretched her sweatshirt into huge shapes denoting pregnancy, and howled at the impossibility of becoming a mother to such a big, demanding child.

I had to say something, or thought I did. "You can take little steps—don't wait for her every time."

"I can't stand the way she looks at me, as if she is dying. And sometimes she comes into our room and just *stands* there and doesn't say anything."

Yes, indeed. Even at this age a guest could be a hanger-on who prevented the hostess from getting her work done.

It seemed Tuttle had fallen in love during spring vacation. This was what had caused her to revolt against a close friendship she had shown every evidence of enjoying. "I wish I could get married," she wept. "My lover is twenty-five. Older men know how to do things."

186

"You have to learn to shake the People-Eaters or you will have them all your life, married or not." But I felt sorry for Chace also. She was not going to find anyone who could "make it up" to her. The hostility she felt against Tuttle when Tuttle would not take care of her was naked and obnoxious; Chace was out to devour Tuttle and didn't know it. I kept on at Tuttle; if she could only see that she gave her full cooperation to all this!

"I am so afraid of being *selfish!*" she howled.

"You remind me of a cartoon I once saw, where the heroine is tied to a railroad track with the train whistling down at full speed, and the villain in his trench coat and black fedora is leering over her. The lady says, "'I'm sorry for you, Gerald, because you are sick.'"

Tuttle laughed. "Do try being selfish, just a little bit," I said.

I remembered that Chace had gone on a date to the Dartmouth Winter Carnival and returned to inform us that her date was a jerk.

"What kind of jerk?"

"Just a *plain jerk*. Terribly conceited." Conceit was not a fault in either Chace or Tuttle; Chace was unsure of herself, and Tuttle was too sympathetic to say "No." I had heard Chace, one other Sunday afternoon, talking to a great Teddy bear of a boy who had a deep voice that sounded as if he were the Papa bear. They were having a conversation, the kind where sex seemed not to be the object. Their voices sounded adult and relaxed; I heard the word *interpretation*. Talk drifted in a vague exploratory fashion as if time did not exist. Chace was sitting on an end table swinging one leg. The Teddy bear boy, who had a blonde thatch for hair, was sprawled on a couch. The conversation was a happening between friends. I was surprised to hear Chace conversing.

My memory of Chace and Tuttle stretched back to autumn when Tuttle, a patient, dear person who came in from beer-drinking expeditions quite maudlin on the subject of herself, howled out her first worry over Chace.

"I can't say *No* to anyone!" she cried. "And I am so sad, and I feel as if worms are under my skin and I have to get *out* of it!" It was impossible to convince Tuttle that even if on one occasion her father had called her a selfish bitch, she was precisely the opposite.

"She won't even go to the dining room alone," she wailed to me.

Chace had large soft brown eyes and masses of long flying hair that got in her face. Her mouth was generous, and when she burst in the door, the air was fractured by yells, followed by bashful grins. If a pixie could grow big and bellow, that would be Chace. She wore blue jeans, dark sweatshirts and old ragged sweaters.

She was the child of parents getting a divorce, and she could not, as Ellen did, find a way of expressing her emotions over eruptions in the family. But Chace, like Ellen, loved her father deeply; when he came for Parents Weekend, on the evening of the Fathers' and Daughters' dance, she appeared downstairs in a lovely black velvet dress with a white lace collar, and long black pantyhose that showed her graceful legs.

She looked a long time at her image in the big plate glass mirror that hung across the hall from my bedroom door, and I stood in my door and looked also, thinking that the dark beauty of Chace, when she revealed it, was worthy of Velasquez.

"Do I look like a girl?" she asked in this moment when we were alone, and the sight of herself made her surprised enough to speak.

"You *are* a girl. If there is any doubt, you can take off your clothes and prove it."

She laughed, and I lost the fear of her shyness, which made me afraid to speak to her for fear she would retreat. She looked out from her masses of hair and grinned. There was another Chace I seldom saw, the one who came running in on a Saturday night at two in the morning, all her inhibitions gone, and lay down spread-eagle fashion in the middle of the entrance hall yelling for joy, strong enough to challenge the pain that kept her from talking and made her need Tuttle so much. When Chace did this, her friends, who were saying "Shhhhh," hoisted her up the stairs to bed, and she hollered all the way.

I remembered that when I was in college (that phrase I hear repeated so often by members of my generation) I was neat and

188

poor and engaged to a boy for five years without ever sleeping with him; that I concealed the sickness, the madness, not knowing it was there at all, that I was a "nice girl" who never found out until she was thirty and divorced that there were parts of herself as rash and passionate, as foolhardy and wrong, as any I sometimes saw in Bixby dorm. What I see in the young today is honest dirt and confusion; they are forcing us to recant on our "innocent hypocrisy" and to look at what we never wanted to see. Now I see the world more as they see it, a place where any kind of honesty, however repulsive, may be better than a pleasant facade, "the old fine-fine."

The day of the Huck Finn expedition, Chace and Tuttle returned talking in deep, throaty voices and garbling syllables in what they described as the articulation of "Glinda the Eastern actress." They sounded as if this exercise had given them sore throats. They had hitchhiked for ten miles down the road to a boys' prep school, which they found disappointing.

"I thought it would be a fun town, and there was nothing to do. The boys aren't even allowed off campus," Tuttle said with a woeful face.

"I'll bet the boys would be afraid of you and Chace. You are women of the world to them—even if you want to be Huck and Tom."

"We wanted to have an *Adventure*."

"Then why didn't you go up to Hanover?" Loud groans.

"We think Darmouth is boring. Besides, we are banned by some of the houses up there—but maybe there are one or two we haven't hit."

They melted into the upper floors.

This was the end of tomboy adventures for Tuttle, for her "lover boy" came to visit later in the spring. On a golden-green afternoon, she waited for him to arrive for the first time since she fell so in love during the spring holiday. He was driving all the way from Michigan and telephoned in the morning to say he would be here by noon. Tuttle was as nervous as a Mexican jumping bean. By 12:20, Tuttle was out in front of the house shouting at the assembled sun-bathers, (who had just howled in chorus, "*Hello*, Mike O'Connor!") "If you do one single thing like that, I am going personally to *kill* you—with my murder stick—I *mean* it!" Barbie stood by her embattled roommate, looking protective but silent. Tuttle had learned to say "No" when she felt like it. She came back in the house, played the piano, drank a Coke, ate cookies, and roamed around like a tigress in her cage which was becoming too small for her. She said they might "camp out." I thought camping out sounded more like fun than huddling in a car or going to a motel. She said also that Mike O'Connor had a tent. I got so nervous myself, responding to Tuttle's vibrations, that I yelled at the girls, "Do behave as if you had seen a man before." They looked startled, then took on a "silly-old-mother" expression, and turned their backs to me like offended cats, slathering on suntan oil in place of licking their paws.

I must have gone out the back door when Mike O'Connor drove up the front drive, for I never did see him. Barbie said that Tuttle took off with the speed of light and jumped into his car. Nothing more was seen of her until she came back radiating love, then lapsed into a depressive gloom composed of loneliness and papers to write. Tuttle had changed from being a sad clown to being a woman in love; this metamorphosis is as common and as magical as a caterpillar turning into a shimmering butterfly, and I could not blame Tuttle for revolting at the academic life, a crawling journey.

The themes of springtime emerged, with twining variations: love and sex, poetry, green leaves, protest. Chace became more independent and one evening she and Barbie decided they must finish a paper on Matthew Arnold for "Brit. Lit."—a prospect they felt was like eating sawdust amid fields of ambrosia.

We settled down and began digging into the resonant, dense prose of circa 1850. I could see why the students were trying to abolish this kind of reading, but they reminded me of athletes who did not want their exercise—their reading muscles were remarkably flabby. The essay was "The Function of Criticism." Chace was very astute and left off her customary antics, but Barbie, who preferred to do chemistry experiments, found Arnold unreadable.

I attempted an explanation of Arnold's poem, "Dover Beach," in an effort to bring him up-to-date.

"The poem ends, 'Ah, love, let us be true to one another,' for Arnold felt that the world was a 'Darkling plain, beset by armies,' and today we are in the same predicament."

"Was this guy in *love?*" Chace inquired with astonishment. She could not conceive that anyone who was in love could write such ponderous poetry.

"Those Victorian gentlemen were wilder than you think," I said.

I tried to compare Arnold's essay on criticism to a review by Walter Kerr on a play like "Hair."

"Arnold says that if the critic is disinterested, he will not criticize a work of art because he has a political axe to grind or for any practical purpose, but he will criticize it in terms of how good it is as an art form and this can lead to new and fresh ideas."

Barbie said, "What is *disinterested?*"

"Impartial, unprejudiced."

Barbie said, "No wonder I couldn't get it. I thought *disinterested* meant he wasn't interested."

Chace said, "I don't see how a critic can know whether a work of art is good or bad."

It was a rugged session. In my hand I was holding a copy of the nineteenth century essayists which I had used in college in 1929, and I had a futile feeling about the educational system. I might as well have been talking a foreign language from a country they had never seen, and examining every work in a dictionary labeled "Past and Present."

We labored over the words *lyric* and *epic* as applied to poetry, and I tried to explain that in England in the nineteenth century, the writers were in rebellion against materialism as exemplified in the Industrial Revolution, and against the conquest of weaker countries by the British Empire.

191

"Don't you see that they were against some of the same things you are—poverty, and Vietnam?"

"Well, why doesn't he *say* so?" Chace said unreasonably. "I don't like him."

Barbie was more philosophical. "I wonder what *our* children will be like?"

The old order was done for in a way that was never quite like this before.

With Chace on the house council, Tuttle on the Dean's List, and Britt completely gone, I wondered what we should do for exuberance? I need not have given this a second thought.

Chace did a series of handstands on the hall rug and said *she* should be on the Dean's List for doing handstands so well. Perhaps she should have been honored for yelling louder than anyone else and going out the door singing, "Come out and play with me," so enthusiastically that her friends couldn't resist answering.

On one occasion Chace succeeded in getting Willie to be the Mother of the Day. I was sitting on the front stoop, a homely word to describe an entrance enhanced by dignified white Greek columns. Sprawled in happy disarray on the lawn and front walk were girls garlanded with sun reflectors, and with the rest of their anatomy as bare as decency and the dean would allow. They glistened with oil, and lay in half-comatose abandon on their backs with their legs forming V's, murmuring to each other or sleeping.

In vain had numerous bulletins requested the girls to sunbathe on the back campus of a Saturday afternoon; they knew all too well that cars full of boys cruised the front drive, and the spectacle of a semicircle of dorms with sunbathing females in bright bikinis would rejoice the hearts looking for dates. Chace, however, had other ideas.

On the front walk, Willie was rolling a shopping center steel cart up and down. Chace was in the shopping cart, wedged tightly, for it was barely big enough for a two-year old. Chace had her head back on the steering bar, and was grinning like a contented infant. Willie, who was too tall to fold herself up to such a small dimension, ran as fast as she could, her steel-rimmed glasses and streaming blonde hair making her look like a cross between an English nanny and a high school kid gone wild.

Both of them screamed, "It's a magic bus!" I looked on in a state of shock. Before long they hauled the shopping cart into the house, and I heard Barbie saying severely, "You can't play with that because it belongs to somebody else."

"*We found it.*" There were more howls and the shopping cart came rolling back out, with such force that it dumped over, and Chace emerged miraculously unscathed. She jumped up and went into the house and began playing the piano, "I've Grown Accustomed to Your Face," then she sang loudly as she played "To Dream the Impossible Dream."

Hypnotized by the warm sun, the illusion of the beach, the air seeming to hang still, I wondered fleetingly, is the impossible dream for Chace to find the permanent, ever-loving, perfect mother who will never leave, never punish? I went inside.

I never worried about Chace. She had brains and made her grades; when exam time came, she studied with her *own* mortar board on her head. I felt Chace would make it in the outside world. Under all her acting-out, there was a really honest person, a tough person I respected.

The Perils of Love

We had songs.
> "Cherry Valley, here I come,
> Right back where I started from."

A little more explicit: "It's a fucking time of year."
And we still had,
> "Come out and play with me,
> And bring your dollies three,
> Climb up my apple tree."

These expressions of sentiment did seem to sum up the emotional range of private recreation, unless you counted the Saturday night movie. Everyone was as mad as the March hare. Lovers arrived, lovers fought, lovers made up. Girls without lovers pined and studied fiercely. For the sake of Auld Lang Syne, I remembered being all dressed up in a grey spring suit, a pink blouse, stockings, heels and seed pearls to sit in a place called a "date parlor" and do some surreptitious necking—under all that decor, my emotions were as passionate as Carmen's; but we had an unholy fear of pregnancy, a prospect that conjured up total disgrace with The Family and visions of

194

Lillian Gish turned out into a snowstorm. An orgasm? I never heard the word, and was as inhibited as my tight skirt.

Now spring exploded in laughter, camping, furies, tears—the Life Force. The noise was awful and the feet pounded incessant rhythms. The spring musical show was *Stop the World, I Want to Get Off,* and I was in agreement; yet to be honest, my emotions rose as if to wild bongo drums.

Fannie, who apparently managed to contrast Antigone and Cordelia, had a marathon heart and soul talk with her boy friend, Merton, all one afternoon. I could hear them in the living room, muttering in tense voices, and at one point, she became hysterical, and ran halfway upstairs with Merton after her. I put her in my sitting room by herself when I found her out on the back doorstep in her bare feet, rocking back and forth and hugging herself in a transport of grief.

I tried to speak to Merton, who was sitting by himself with his hair so far over his face that I could not see how he felt. The girls said that Merton looked like a grasshopper; he was long and bony. Whatever was the matter with Fannie and Merton they talked for so many hours that they exacerbated their wounds. Why is love so hard to learn about?

I went up to Fannie's room and got Celia, her roommate, who was tall and kind, but when Celia came down, Fannie turned into a little tigress and screamed at her to stay out of it. Then Fannie and Merton went out to the car where they yelled at each other until the dorm next door called up and asked me to put a stop to the noise. I went out and got them back in the house, where they were still at it for hours into the evening.

Virgie, as might have been expected, took her ups and downs with all the drama of a Carol Burnett. One Saturday evening, I felt that life was becoming too complicated, with spring bursting out both the leaves and the girls faster than fireworks, for with a "mixer" going on in the gym, boys swarmed in and out of the house at every moment, some drunk, some sober, some courteous, and some boorish. But at 11:30 Brandie, Willie, and Buffy came into my sitting room armed with books, mugs of coffee, Cokes and crackers, and said they would like to settle down in there to write their papers for "Brit.

Lit." I was not able to understand how a group of people could write papers together.

I was going to bed, so I said, "Fine. When the drunks come rolling in, will you please tell them to enjoy life quietly."

Brandie said with a wicked grin, "We will say, 'Be quiet, for our house mother is asleep.'"

"You will not," I said. "Tell them to be quiet because you are writing a Brit. Lit. paper and you cannot concentrate on analyzing two poems for eight pages unless you can hear yourself think."

It was around 1:30 that the action went into second gear. I was in bed, quietly drowsing, when I heard the commotion that is called "getting the boys to go home." Voices were announcing that the clock was fast and they *really* had two more minutes, as if two minutes were all the difference between life and death. Five minutes went by, then I opened my door and found a very drunk boy sitting outside my door on the hall settle.

"I'm sorry, but you will have to leave—or the girl you are with will be the one to get campused next weekend."

He was a happy, silent drunk, and he got up amiably and staggered to the front door. Then out of the corner of my eye, I saw three girls scuttling around like hysterical chickens, and Virgie rushed in howling and screaming. At the top of her vocal powers, she was crying, "Why? Why? Why? He was just *using* me."

I was not really daunted, for alcohol frequently produced weird effects, and it was warm enough for everyone to be intoxicated to begin with, so I went into my room and left Virgie to the tender ministrations of her friends.

But the screaming continued. I could hear Virgie sobbing. I thought of tranquilizers, but no, that would mean going to the infirmary, and even if Virgie sounded insane, she really was not. So I got up and went out again. Pat had Virgie in the living room and stood there with this wailing banshee, looking helpless. I took Virgie in my arms, and she cried like a large baby, her mascara running down her cheeks in rivulets of black salt water.

Virgie, our big, blooming cabbage rose, felt solid and strange in my arms, as if I were trying to comfort someone more

196

durable than I. Between her incoherent yowls, I learned that our favorite boy friend, Jake (who had succeeded in changing Virgie from a big tomboy into a blushing and palpitating female), had taken another girl to the mixer.

I made mumbling sounds about how Jake would be back, and anyway, that Virgie must learn that men do things like this, and so do women.

But all Virgie would say was "Why? Why? Why?" in hysterical tones of disillusionment.

At last three girls shepherded her down to the Butt, where I could hear the howling continuing with all the fervor of a grief-stricken wife at the wailing wall. Brandie and her cohorts had vacated my sitting room, leaving the floor covered with books and Coke bottles; obviously they planned to return when the storm ceased.

But Barbie had heard. She came downstairs, looking as lovely as one's mother did a great many years ago, and dressed in a bright green silk nightgown. She stood in the middle of the front hall with the lights from the chandelier gleaming on her reddish blonde hair, and considered the crisis calmly.

Virgie screamed from downstairs, "It hurts, it hurts, it hurts! It hurts right here in my stomach."

"What a healthy girl," I said to Barbie. I envied Virgie, for I could never remember a time when I could cry like that except in privacy. But Virgie, with her instinct for a lusty life lived up to the hilt, was not going to stop unless we stopped her.

Barbie was holding her stomach. "I know how it hurts, I know just how she feels. I guess I will have to *do* something," she said, and she went back upstairs.

I went back in my room again, but after awhile I heard laughing, so I got up for the last time. The Brit. Lit. crowd was back in my sitting room, rolling over among their books with glee. Barbie was standing in the door in an old pink terry cloth bathrobe with a big hole in it, the most unwashed, dirty old robe I ever saw, and she had taken out an artificial tooth I had never known she possessed. She was grinning like a six-year-old with the hole in her smile, and she said, "Tuttle says she is going to burn up this robe. Well, O.K., but I took out my tooth and put this robe on, and now everything seems to be better."

The phone was ringing. I took it off the hook and said without waiting to hear of the latest excitement, "Call the dean."

Virgie's sense of humor was equal to her furies, and before long, Jake returned for keeps. She was in love in a shining way, and every evening she collected half a dozen girls to go to Jake's, also a few boys lying around on the floor waiting for some action. Jake was a bachelor who had his own house. Virgie's masses of blonde hair flew out from her shoulders in a bright nimbus, and she sang. She wanted all of us to share her joy, and when Jake came in with his two St. Bernards, even these immense dogs seemed infected with Virgie's exuberance. One almost knocked me over.

"Don't you *all* want to go to Jake's?" Virgie would cry. "Mrs. Martin, don't *you* want to go with us to Jake's?" Dear Virgie.

On a sunny afternoon, Virgie cavorted around outdoors, yelling wild insults at the dorm next door. "Hey, Oliver! Your mother sweeps a pay toilet!"

What followed was a chorus of noises.

"I can't study!"

"A bug is on my goddam nose."

"I had a beetle up my shirt one time and you know where?"

"I'm uncomfortable!"

I could hear a transistor radio droning hymns on an organ.

"Yoohoo!!! You with the pink Cadillac!"

In all this Virgie's voice again, "Where's my singing stuff? I wanna sing to my roommate."

Virgie was married to Jake that summer.

Maria's love life was more complicated and laced with dark and light, a black boy who loved her madly, and a white boy she was never quite sure of; they aroused in her conflicting emotions.

Maria's black boy friend, Louis, called up and told her he was going to commit suicide by jumping off the Prudential

Building in Boston. He said he had been up there several times and the glass was thin and he would go right through it. Louis was a Vietnam veteran at age twenty-three; he had seen a Vietnamese girl slit his buddy's throat in an airplane and he shot the girl's head off. He was violently upset because Maria was in love with a white boy.

Maria looked desperate. "He is messing up my mind," she said. We went into my bedroom and I got the college psychiatrist on the phone for Maria. He told her to notify Louis' parents. But Maria felt she had to call Louis first, and he begged her not to do this. Finally he said, "I'm glad you care." Maria hung up the phone.

"He's been on drugs and he has threatened to kill me. He *hates* white people."

"I can only grieve and write to congressmen, dear Maria."

Maria went over and ensconced herself in my easy chair, where she sat writing poetry and brooding over Danny, her white lover at Dartmouth, who hadn't shown up for a long time. She showed me a poem called "The Soul Ant."

"What does *soul* mean, anyway?" I asked.

"It means black, black food, black music, think black about everything." In the poem, the soul ant was crossing the floor with his "brown head uptight" and Maria was sitting on the john.

"As I shat," she wrote, "I lifted up my brown-and-white saddle shoe for the uptight crunch." It was a vivid and arresting poem. Maria needed the word *brown* to express her own color; the boys from the Afro-American Society at Dartmouth had driven her into an examination of her feelings. And there was poor, shocked Louis. Danny, who blew hot and cold, had been challenged on the dance floor by some of the black brothers at Dartmouth, for they resented having Maria in love with a white man.

Now she fell to talking about Danny. "I don't know whether he is good enough for me or not. He never comes to hear me sing. And he had his hometown honey up for Green Key."

We sat in silence for a moment. "The girls didn't seem to understand how I could be up early and working in the cafeteria the same as always after the night I sang 'Carmen.'" Naturally. After the concert and the party, Maria walked in and gave the loudest and most rolling *burp* I have ever heard in my life.

Three members of the Afro-American Society visited us, and I talked with one of them, a tall black boy in a red sweater with a silver chain around his neck. He told me they were here to "make an appraisal." I presumed this was a preliminary gesture to determine whether we were worth reforming.

"I think we are," I said aloud now to Maria. Maria looked at me and laughed. The girls never asked for explanations of such mental short-circuits.

I felt impelled to explain, however. "I was just thinking about that letter you wrote to the Afro-American Society." Maria laughed. "Boy, were they mad when I asked them if I could ask some white people to join! But I signed my letter, 'Yours in the struggle, man.'" She was bent on going to Yale to study drama, and her love life was tumultous, sophisticated, peripheral.

Lisa! Bright spring! April sun and a cold wind. Lisa was now happy, for Larry kissed her at last. He made of her a well woman and they were going to get married, but Lisa, while becoming quiet and easy to live with, had three academic warnings.

Wearing a big plaid boy's cap and a false moustache, she swatted Les on the behind, saying, "Now do what Mother says." Les made little whimpering noises. Les and Lisa had something in common—Mother. During vacation, Lisa's mother boomed the whole length of Saks' in Boston, "Why don't you answer when I'm calling you?"

I have scarcely mentioned Madeleine, for she was one of those people like warm bread who are so comfortable that we take them for granted. She was honest, gentle, and strong. And she was in love with a boy who was in the army and had been ordered overseas.

200

But I was not impressed with Madeleine's parents, who arrived unannounced one night while I was in my sitting room hashing over with some of the girls the study questions for Brit. Lit. While we sat innocently inquiring into *The Wasteland*, Mr. and Mrs. Grindley were creating it out front. They tackled the permission slips we kept filed by the sign-out book and took one that showed Madeleine had signed out for a motel the night before Barry, her fiance, went overseas.

Madeleine came to the door and asked for Barbie some hours later. The Grindleys had dragged her over to the art center for a "dressing down," doing away with her study time and completely disrupting her emotions.

Barbie returned in a blazing fury. "They are going to use the overnight slip as evidence against her."

"Evidence of *What?*" It sounded like a court case.

"I don't know." Barbie sat down with an unusual expression of disgust on her face.

Madeleine came to me later. She was in tears.

"They used every old cliché there is. I am now a fallen woman because I went to a motel. They have not raised me to be immoral. They forbade me to write to him, and he will be away a year and a half. I didn't do anything wrong," she said, weeping, "I just didn't know any other way to be alone with him, and he was so sad about leaving."

"I know you didn't do anything wrong if you felt it was right," I said. I was furious. The whole thing seemed so stupid, especially now that Barry was gone.

The Grindleys went to a motel themselves and called up twice to find out how Madeleine was reacting.

"What will your friends think of you?" they said. When Madeleine told me this, I laughed. "Tell them the friends take overnight permissions and go where they please." I was embarrassed for her parents.

What the Grindleys accomplished was to lose Madeleine, who had never been able to challenge them, but now she would. She was twenty years of age.

201

The next evening we went back to T.S. Eliot. Brandie read from her notes. "The wasteland is a place where there is no fertility and everything has dried up—culture, creation, civilization, and everything has become materialistic—it is a dead place. Just think, he wrote it in 1922. I guess that is why he was then in the avant garde."

Perhaps a cure for parents who were "mixed-up old people" would be to read what their children were reading and write an exam on it. How could parents be resurrected if they didn't know they were behaving as if they were dying?

"It all takes place between a Good Friday and Easter Sunday," Ellen said. "And the Fisher King is the crucified source of life—but he is part man. And I think Eliot had hope, because the Hindu words at the end mean, 'Give, sympathize, control.'"

"What kind of control?"

"Yourself and the bad things in people."

I gave out at eleven, and they went on until three in the morning, patiently trudging their way over the hard terrain of Eliot and his erudition. What energy they had! If they didn't understand, they wore themselves out trying.

Midnight. The front hall crawling with unattached boys, who wanted to sit on the floor, the tables, to watch the passing parade. There were too many of them and they viewed me always as someone to avoid, a prowling member of the police force. My sitting room was full of girls watching Marilyn Monroe in *Some Like It Hot*. My bedroom was attractive because I wanted to go to bed, but if I got undressed and then had to go out in the hall, I would be conspicuous, for I did not share the girls' slap-happiness about appearing socially in a nightgown, robe, and slippers.

These boys, I reminded myself, were not all that different from the boys reading their angry or sexy poems at Richard Eberhart's, where I was a harmless lady; but here the word *chaperone* hung in the air, menacing as a tarantula. Yet we seemed to have more boys than any other dorm, rumor had it; a dorm of two hundred girls struck them as a bit chilly. "Those places are like a *motel*," the girls said.

202

Well, I could not change my outward image, and feeling irritated I went up to Barbie's and Tuttle's room and we had a go at discussing modern poetry. The room looked like a chaotic closet, with clothes everywhere, and Barbie came in and began putting these away in a housewifely fashion.

I sat in the easy chair and Tuttle sat cross-legged on Barbie's bed in her famous position where she crossed her legs and kept her feet turned up on the outside at the same time. Barbie curled up on the foot of the bed. It was cozy. We ended by reading Auden's "Lay your sleeping head, my love,/ Human on my faithless arm," and it gave me so much gooseflesh that I quit and went away. The last lines, "Nights of insult let you pass/ Watched by every human love," were impossible to explain except to sophisticated people who knew what life was like. "Faithless arm"? "Nights of insult"? One could not pass all this off by saying Auden was a homosexual; the poem rang true, the gentleness, the bitterness, the *experience*. For a brief moment, I grieved over the past, while Barbie and Tuttle sat there healthy and radiant with all their future opening before them. But they responded; they shivered as if an invisible arrow had pierced the protection of the room. The poem rang in my head all the next day.

When I went back downstairs, the hall had thinned out, and my sitting room door was open. A new species of Boy was looking at the books. He looked forlorn, tall and thin, with long, silky hair and a sensitive face with a curly mouth. What a novelty! A bookish boy right here in this dating bureau at one in the morning!

"Hello," I said. "See anything you like?"

He was quite serious and sat down, holding a copy of Kafka, *The Trial*. "Lots. You have some good stuff."

My ego rose ten points. He said he was from Dartmouth via Chicago University.

"Say, I was down in the Butt all by myself in the dark. I hope you don't mind my coming in here—I see why the girls call that place 'the ghetto.'" He had a flat midwestern voice, but the words came out smoothly, easily.

Les came to the door, peeped in, and went away. Shy, elfin Les.

"What's your name?" I said.

"Bromley. Say, that girl must have the longest hair I've seen."

"Oh, *hair!*" I said. "It seems to be a protective veil. Your hair is beautiful, you know. Hair is sexy, isn't it?" He laughed and looked less forlorn, more comfortable.

"Yes, I guess so. Now there is clean hair, dirty hair, red hair, black hair, blonde hair, pubic hair, hair on the chest—but *any* hair is better than none, isn't it? It's to feel, to get your hands in, to rumple, to wash, to fly around, to grow on your face if you want a beard or a moustache—hair is *great*. It's the only thing you can *change*, unless you are fat and want to go on a diet. You can wash it, dye it, cut it off, or just sit and hide in it."

He pushed his hands through his own hair.

"Yours looks clean, shiny. But you don't have a beard. The other day a girl said, 'I love my hair—I'm vain about it. I want it to grow way down to my hips.' She's a girl who thinks she is not pretty and hates to look at the mean old lady on 'Laugh-In,' the one who wears a hair net and hits the old man with her purse."

"Freudian as hell," he said. "But she's right. Hair is exciting to *feel.*"

"I'm really tired of TV ladies who advertise shampoo with 'flashing eyes and floating hair,'" I grumbled. Then I yawned. It was 1:30 by my watch.

"Only 'Kubla Khan' was an opium dream. The TV was *awful* tonight. But say, how about 'He that hath a beard is more than a youth, and he that hath no beard is less than a man.'" He was grinning with mischief. "Am I less than a man?"

I blinked. "You've got me," I said.

"Shakespeare. Beatrice. Say, have you got any girls for a guy like me?"

"I doubt it. You'll have to find out for yourself." I was thinking of Brandie, of Ellen, but if I began fixing up dates I would end up in the trash barrel from sheer disintegration. "Do come back any time," and I got up. "It's been a joy to meet you."

He shook hands gravely and walked out into the night, whistling a sprightly tune I could hear drifting away down the street like pollen from apple blossoms.

204

In my youth, Sunday was the hardest day in the week, and I thought it was because my father was a minister. In Bixby dorm, Sunday was a day when we could breathe. It was the only morning in the week when Mrs. Perley did not come and there were no classes; the only morning when I could awaken to silence and know that breakfast would be changed to brunch at 9:30.

In the afternoon, the tempo picked up. One afternoon I was lying on my bed enjoying Sunday, surrounded by the flood of newspaper called the *New York Times*. It was sleepy and comfortable. Callers were coming and going outside, and I could almost imagine it was like the Sundays of my youth in one respect—in the afternoon, the church next door rested, and everyone in the house took a nap.

Gradually I became aware that there was a congregation in the living room, for I heard a boy saying, "I always remember a girl by her hair." The boys were honey bees exploring.

I couldn't tell how many people were in the living room, but someone began reading from the Wadleigh 1937 songbook, and the group shouted in unison, "*Drink* a pink martini to Wadleigh," then laughed. Chace's husky voice came on, and she said she didn't get very drunk last night; then the boys began a post mortem on how drunk some of their dates got in thirty seconds.

"Wow, mine was climbing all over me." A laughing, satisfied voice.

"I won't have any more blind dates—I don't like them *fat*." Sadly, "I passed out."

Les, who had a distinctive purity about sex, began reading the comics in a loud voice. I imagined her sitting on the floor immersed in a screen of newspaper, a pale, conservative hippie enveloped in her cape of hair.

"They were pinching behinds and I gave somebody a black eye every time." Les sounded as if she was holding her nose. "Animals!"

The animals erupted with violence. They were singing "Fight for the right of Wadleigh/And kill those little green bugs!" The tempo was rising as the hours waned toward evening.

The boys resumed their sexual exploration by means of leading questions. Soft feminine voices parried with answers. Everyone laughed. The girls had immense patience with the delicate male ego, a seductive set of maneuvers designed to keep things pleasant but mysterious. On Sunday afternoon, the heavy scene was somewhere else.

"What do you do when you are hot?"

"We sweat it out or go up to Dartmouth."

I was beginning to believe what I had been told, that Dartmouth was the second horniest college on the East coast; who held first place, I never found out.

There was a little silence, as if the conversation was becoming too intimate for the big, cool living room with its greens and blues, its chintz draperies with designs of Grecian urns and the high windows open to spring. The living room had an almost gracious air at times.

"Let's go downstairs to the Butt—it's real cute down there."

"What's the Butt?"

"It means cigarette butt, and not what you think. Come on."

Tramping feet past my door. A few boys lagged behind to read the weekly menu on the bulletin board.

"Eggs Benedict for brunch—aw, come *on*, now."

At least they did not laugh at Virgie's paper which was posted to show that she had finally got an A, with the comment on it by Virgie, "Hey fellas, look at this."

I seldom went down to the Butt. It was under my bedroom, and when the TV blared up like a subterranean blasting after midnight, I went down and stood there half asleep, until we reached an agreement about our ears. The Butt was dark and often dotted with empty Coke cans, bits of candy wrappers, left-over crumbs of potato chips and crackers. It was gloomy, with basement windows high in the wall covered by dark green curtains, and institutional plastic-covered lounges and chairs— on the whole, a rather dead testament to the youthful preference for chaos. The standing ash trays would have been at home

206

in a rundown Victorian hotel catering to traveling salesmen, and there was a metal garbage can for butts. To add to the atmosphere, the girls had moved the ironing board in there so they could iron and look at TV, like bored housewives. I was intrigued to hear it called "real cute."

They were now settled there. "Thanks a lot!" someone was yelling.

Maria had remained behind in the living room and was playing some good, solid hymns on the battered grand piano, "Rock of Ages," and "A Mighty Fortress Is Our God," and singing in her lovely, sweet voice. The lines of my parsonage past intersected in the air with the noise from the Butt. I opened my door just as Tuttle came downstairs dressed in her whacked-off blue jeans and a white shirt. A round face, half lonely, half ironically amused, with a smooth patina of innocence and wisdom.

"Can I borrow your scissors?" she said. "I'm going to get my hair cut."

I gave her the scissors, and a few minutes later, I followed her down to the Butt to find a scene of domestic tranquility. In the glare of overhead fluorescent lights that illuminated the Butt like a scene from the Living Theatre, the unattached males were comfortably slouched in and over chairs, smoking or drinking Cokes; couples were holding hands, and Barbie had Tuttle sitting on a stool while she cut her hair with all the fond care of a good mother.

When I came into the dorm at three o'clock of another Sunday afternoon, I noticed three girls sitting on the floor of the living room in a hushed silence that reminded me of a religious meeting. There were a few strange murmurs such as I had never heard the girls making before, but I could not see what was inspiring this unusual reaction, so I went to the door and peered in. A *baby*, that was all. A baby about eight months old, who was introduced as the nephew of Beatrice. He was a baby for the Gerber ads, with large dark eyes, a very round head, and tiny hands and feet.

Barbie was bouncing the baby and he looked delighted. What he wanted was to stand up, like every human being since the time of the apes. But he had to be held up to stand, and then fought against sitting down by bracing his pigmy legs hard on the floor.

I held the baby and smelled the back of his neck and kissed his soft, petal-like cheeks. I knew what the girls were feeling. Sentimentalism? Perhaps so, but the physical feeling of a baby certainly beats holding a Teddy bear.

"It's a *baby*," someone said foolishly. Chace picked him up and held him gently, then took him over to the piano and struck a few soft notes.

Buffy sat on the back of the sofa and looked adoring; everyone else sat on the floor doing likewise. Vicki studied the baby with a loving yet professional eye, like a pediatrician. I got the baby some wooden beads and some little plastic cowboys and Indians, which he promptly chewed, then he grinned, displaying two tiny front teeth.

"Oh, he has teeth!"

I sat and remembered my own babies, looking at them when they were brought to me for the first time, unwrapping the hospital blanket to see if they had everything they were supposed to have; I checked over their little bodies as carefully as a mother cat does. My own mother had told me not to worry "if their legs and arms were on straight." They were. Later on I sometimes wondered about their heads.

The baby stayed with us all afternoon and never cried. He drank orange juice, had his diapers changed, and finally lay in his carrying basket down in the Butt while his parents looked at TV.

"He loves TV," his mother said.

Beatrice said decisively, "Children under five years of age should not look at TV."

"Well, he is bewitched by it," his mother said.

"I wonder which of us will have a baby first?" one girl said with longing.

Everyone looked aghast. I think at least half of those present were taking the pill.

"Please, not *now*," someone else said. But the baby was the only person who had ever made them all quiet. A few boys came in, looked at the baby, and what they saw made them look scared and reflective.

Barbie came in one day to tell me she had been to the "Spring Retreat" and the students were suggesting changes; one was that the boys should be allowed upstairs in the girls' rooms the next year from noon until midnight on weekends. Having the boys visit upstairs was called having *parietals*, and this was a new word to me, so I looked it up.

Parietals meant (rare) "living within, or having to do with life within, a college." It came from *paries, parietis*, Latin, meaning *a wall*. The theme song for all this could be, "And the walls came tumbling down." What they wanted was no walls between the sexes.

The anatomical definition of *parietals* is "of the parities, or walls of a hollow organ, cavity, cell, etc.; especially designating either of the two bones between the frontal and occipital bones, forming part of the top and sides of the skull."

In botany, "attached to the wall of the ovary, as the placenta in some plants." Ah, that was more like it.

Apparently the girls felt we needed parietals to keep our heads and ovaries organized. But these were walls, not the absence of walls. The girls felt that in life within the college, we needed to move the walls back.

The student body president was promoting a six-weeks trial period. "They will get what they want," Barbie said. "Don't worry, I'll hang in there upstairs."

I had a cowardly fit over parietals. "Why don't you have the trial period in *winter*?" I asked.

"Oh, come *on*!" Barbie said.

I had to admit that when my father got so adamant about making me get in at midnight, I got angry and told him I would do nothing after midnight that I could not do at five o'clock in the afternoon. He had somehow classified what he thought was sin by the hour of the clock. Sin and sex were now not so related as they used to be. Sex, for people with healthy minds and bodies, had come up in the world to being a respectable and universal pleasure, but it was still dynamite.

We had meetings at the dean's house. The dean sighed over three in the morning and six also. "I would be up all night." She was right. But finally the president, who had been subjected to a wallowing tide of protests and demands on the subject of Letting the Boys Visit in the Rooms, accepted the demands which were approved by the faculty, gave a beautiful high tea at his home for the seniors, and called a meeting at ten that evening.

It was over—but one-thirty was to be the limit. His speech was formal, explicit. It was a disappointment to a small contingent of girls who wanted a fight. After the meeting, the Bixby dorm girls stamped in, sat down on the floor, and said he was great. Barbie was jumping with glee and clapping her hands on her old beat-up overalls.

"You ought to see those kids, all those kids who have been stirring up the fuss. Boy, are they *furious!* It was just like they were pushing on the door of his office and he opened it and said, 'Come in, ladies,' and they all fell flat on their faces."

I was wrong to be apprehensive about parietals. I am of the generation who was brought up to think, but never quite believed, that if boys visited girls in their rooms, all hell would break loose. Exactly why we thought this, I have no idea. When the boys went upstairs, I heard feet running back and forth, and voices yelling. I was also gratified to find the girls cleaning their rooms every weekend. I was never of the opinion that sexual intercourse among the young and unmarried was more likely to take place surrounded by dozens of noisy friends; it would take place in a variety of ways known to history. If this be treason, anyone is free to make the most of it.

Every weekend in that green spring, the boys trooped up to the girls' rooms for the Great Experiment. They still seemed a bit shy about going up, and the cry was heard, "Man on the floor!" By 4:45 of a Friday afternoon, there was great excitement. In place of the subtle and electric hush of serious sex in the making, I heard what sounded like a French comedy. It has always seemed to me that the French know sex is fun. And even

210

a person as "old" as I was remembered that sex is an ambience of joy and not only something you read about in sex manuals.

I heard the boys and girls chasing each other up and down the halls with cheerful stamping and shouting. They seemed to be trying on each other's clothes.

"Oh, aren't you *pretty!*"

"Virgie, give me that shirt *right now*," Jake's voice demanded with heavy authority.

"I've been wearing this for the past three months," Virgie yelled in a gravelly voice. I heard screams and thudding sounds of wrestling.

In any case, there were no sticky inhibitions, or if these existed, they had taken themselves to the library or home to mother. Fannie and Celia had a batik bedspread hung on a curtain rod over their door. Did this mean, "Come in," or "Stay out?"

I bought for Barbie and Tuttle the last word in American nonessential manufactures, two bright pink foam rubber doorknob covers which, they said on the package, would do an amazing number of things for the owners, including eliminating electric shocks caused by walking on rugs.

When I gave these to Barbie, she yelled at the absurdity and put them on her ears. We tried them on doorknobs and found they surpassed anything we had ever felt in the way of phony tactile sensation; they squished under our hands. "Just the thing for parietals!" Barbie yelled. If the current trend in foam rubber kept up, someone would manufacture a whole foam rubber woman.

A *Rite of Spring*

I stood in the door of my sitting room one evening during noisy hour and decided I was a slum dweller. The living room and the bicycle room were parking lots; the kitchen was the snack bar; and the laundry room was the laundromat. The luggage room was the storage and moving company; the Butt was the neighborhood pool hall. Up and down the narrow streets the neighbors ran in and out among their little, messy houses, or played in the alleys among the garbage cans. The paint was peeling from the walls. My room with its books was the public library. The whole place at ten o'clock was littered with empty Coke bottles and candy wrappers, shoes, jackets, and books.

When Mrs. Perley came in the morning, the place changed into a refined residence for young ladies. I was ready to give up from sheer fatigue on this beautiful, cool, balmy evening.

But no. Just as we had tidied up the house and I was ready to retire, I heard screams and yells denoting that perhaps a tribe of savages had invaded the campus, and running to the windows, I saw a large, milling crowd of females approaching us with buckets of water. "Water!" they yelled feverishly, "Water! Water!" I did not know that water as a battle cry could produce such a heated effect. Almost instantly, my girls were grabbing metal wastebaskets and buckets and running wildly from the bathrooms to the windows to pour out great splashes upon the heads of the invading forces, who meanwhile threw gallons of water inside wherever they could find an open window.

It was unbelievable, like a fantasy in action, like a weird movie of wet hysterics, like all the Freudian symbols of woman, Aphrodite rising from the drains in a surrealistic form of frustration. I stood inarticulate, then spoke, and no word of mine could stem the tide until finally, I felt the excitement of it. I had to grab a chair to keep from running to seize a bucket of water myself.

Pat was running to the bath with her robe hiked up in her two hands, and girls everywhere were yelling with increasing violence, "Water! Water! Water!" The hall by the back door was soon awash, and several of our more intrepid fighters rushed outside, where the water brigade handed them buckets of water through the windows, while other great torrents of water from the enemy came hurling back on their faces. I thanked technology for indoor-outdoor rugs. I put the drapes as far back as they would go and moved chairs from the line of scrimmage—but no one noticed me; they had gone mad with the delights of wetness. Muddy footprints and water began to cover the hall and the stairs. A girl from another dorm rushed in dressed in a skin-diving suit and helmet, yelling "Where's Barbie?" and galloped up the stairs with a large bucket of water for the special drowning of the president of the house.

This state of siege continued for one hour, and promptly at midnight it ceased. I looked out in the hall and saw Les in big yellow oilskin overalls, drenched as a wet kitten, and Beatrice waving a mop that dripped as she swung it over her head with all the frantic joy of a medieval maiden who had defended her honor valorously. Dripping girls were running around like so many chattering hens caught in a thunderstorm, and one of them said, "We didn't chicken out." They laughed and yelled for another hour, and the house officers began calling "Good night, everyone," at frequent intervals, whereupon ten or so girls would yell, *"Good Night!"* and collapse all over again into screams of giggles.

What was this? The enactment of some primitive birth ritual? The next day after Mrs. Perley and some of the maintenance crew had succeeded in restoring order to the house and I had listened to their comments, tired Mrs. Perley stood before me like a blessing. I never wearied of her. The sun was flooding into the hall from the open doors, and Mrs. Perley, in her pale blue uniform, with her fair hair a bit frowsy and her blue eyes twinkling with a starry humor, resembled a down-to-earth angel.

"The rugs will dry out," she said, "girls will be girls." Then she walked out with her basket and her mop, and I thanked God that Mrs. Perley did not have a philosophy of education.

The most curious aspect of the water fight was that it followed hard upon campus elections—a time of wild competition and celebration—two weeks of petitions, teas, speeches, and voting, culminating in a ritual of secret intensity, the induction of new officers. I had been almost euphoric over the "democracy working" theme; now I mused about whether the girls had a genius for working off their hostilities after behaving in adult fashion for two weeks.

I went out to dinner the next night and thereby missed the greatest and most revolting food fight, according to Elizabeth Wyckoff, the dining room had ever seen. Chocolate pie was the main ammunition, and glasses were broken; the combination of chocolate pie and broken glass was lethal. Girls stood on tables and hurled food until the commons resembled a garbage dump.

The president called the student body together at ten o'clock and addressed them, his voice shaking with anger. Among other things, he told them that he had not "come clean" with himself about them, and he had perhaps been too naive. He confessed to a vague ache in his heart, a sort of general pessimism that cut deep and hurt sharp and undermined faith, and he gave his reasons: the fraud of fake tickets for shows, shoplifting in the stores, drinking on campus, excessive and

214

irresponsible cutting of classes, plagiarism, breaking of state and federal laws. He defined their hypocrisy about phony heroes, about parents, about wrong idols, and he made it plain that he did care.

Some of the girls came back dewy-eyed; others were in a rage. The president was to many of them a kind father; I had the strange impulse to wonder if the boys who were revolting on college campuses needed a woman president?

Pat had volunteered to tell me about the meeting, but all she had to say was, "He cares about us." I was more interested in this than in the copy of his speech which had been given to the adults.

Not all the adults believed the president had a good policy. I was sometimes afflicted with listening to the views of a man on the staff who said with relish that what the girls needed was what they used to give to the boys in a camp where he was a counselor.

"We used to get them and put them through the paddle line. That cured them."

Did it? I recalled that the biography of T. H. White, the author of *The Sword in the Stone,* made it clear that the whippings and beatings in the English public school made him a sadist and a homosexual; this unhappy combination caused him to spend his life in a hopeless knowledge that he could not live without cruelty. He loved falcons, hunting, and bloodshed.

Pat said that Barbie cried while the president was speaking. Then it was Barbie who stood up on the stage and put up her hands in a lifting gesture, bringing everyone to their feet to sing the alma mater. I agreed with Kingman Brewster of Yale; we were trying, some of us, to rediscover our own sons and daughters, and to tell the truth, if we had only water fights and food fights to worry about, we were lucky. What next? I wondered. A cliché! How else to describe the energy, the swift changes of mood in the young?

I did not know then that these events were pale preliminaries to May, 1970.

The Mad Hatter

The left-over leaves from last autumn had lain under the snow these many months. It was Cleaning-Up Time. The men were sweeping up the dead leaves and the fuzzy dead grass into neat little piles and carting the piles off in a truck. The bicycles were all out and cluttered up the basement. The torrents of spring were loose, and the peepers sang their first song in the brooks - and the birds! One forgets birdsong until it returns, and early morning brings the chorus.

I had been saddled with advising the Student Alumni Fund, and one day we met to plan money-making activities. *Deja Vu!* Class rings, caps and gown for rent, a dry cleaning service. A *slave* auction? I was against that, but they were determined until later on when a naive girl approached the dean of the college, who had all the dignity and graciousness of an Eleanor Roosevelt—but she was far more beautiful, well-boned, with a great wit, and a resonant, cultivated voice.

Barbie remarked in one of our conferences, "She is a great lady." In truth, visits to this dean in her office had been for me a respite from the kindly but dull encounters in the administration

216

building; she would have graced the presidency of any women's college in the Ivy League. And she did not suffer fools gladly.

"Would you be auctioned off as a slave?" the naive girl asked shyly.

"I sure as hell would not," the dean replied.

After the shock waves subsided, the organization proceeded just the same, but the slave auction was forbidden the day before it was scheduled.

I wanted to have some entertainment; the spring fever was in my bones, and one day while I was shopping in Concord, I saw a large woven pink straw hat with a big rose on the front. Yes. They would wear it with blue jeans. The girls were ardent exponents of Freud's "hat theory," a simplistic one: hats are a feminine symbol. (What would the great man think of unisex fashions?) They appeared in the dining room in gruesome old pants and sweaters, with large, floppy felt hats on their heads, as well as men's laboring caps, hunters' hats of bright red, or straw creations with brims. And they loved men's old hats, especially derbies or battered felts.

I went home and read in Lewis Carroll, who was the expert of his time on the mad, mad world, and I found the Mad Hatter saying some astute things on the subject. We could have a hat rummage sale.

I unlocked the door to the linen room down in our basement, where I found a big, empty closet. Storing hats was not an easy matter, and I started the collection with three of my own: a huge white, somewhat shapeless straw with a white velvet ribbon I bought at I. Magnin's in San Francisco on a wonderful summer day, when the sun turned the city into a Mediterranean shimmer of blue and bisque; an awful little beige felt I wore to England one summer; and a battered hat of blue and green I hung onto in spite of its dented crown, because it matched a purse. I was hoping that every woman in New Devon owned at least three hats she never wore.

The response was Freudian without a doubt. "A hat rummage sale!" We canvassed Main Street, little villages, the offices, the dorms, and hats came pouring in. Every woman who came to the door listened with dubious surprise. Then I saw a slightly crazy glitter in her eye at the mere thought of seeing so many hats assembled in one place.

I watched Vicki making a gum-wrapper hat through a number of long evenings when she sat by my desk folding the tiny pieces of paper and fastening them together in a long chain. She was a miracle of precision in her handiwork. The long strip was sewn into a coolie hat of many colors, with orange ribbons to tie it on the head.

Chace immediately grabbed it and tried it on; she looked charming in it, with her great dark eyes and long hair. She was determined to have it.

"How much shall I charge for it?" I asked Vicki. She considered seriously and said, "Well, if you count all the time it took to chew the gum—!"

"No fair," I said. So she ventured that three dollars would be enough, but I decided to ask five.

Mr. and Mrs. Littlehale of the Inn were helpful about the hats. "Polly Reilly has the biggest hats in town," Mr. Littlehale said, "and you should see her and Ted in the summer, tooling around in a yellow convertible, with Polly in a big hat."

I went to see Mrs. Reilly, who was my dressmaker, a large, energetic lady who worked in an upstairs bedroom, surrounded by chairs full of dresses, hangers full of dresses, and nondescript piles of materials. I entered by the back door downstairs, where a card said, "Ring the bell and come up." Through the kitchen, up the red-carpeted stairs, and there was Mrs. Reilly. Even the bed with its crocheted spread was a sewing sea. And Polly Reilly sat in her black and white print at her sewing machine, with her lustrous auburn hair held on top of her head by a tortoise shell comb.

"Hello," she said. "My, don't you look nice today?" She was a great tonic for the ego, and ruddy as a Macintosh apple.

I explained about the hats. All the ladies began by telling me their old hats were not good enough; the hats were "Just old wrecks," and besides, they might do them over some day, but they had never got around to it. The truth was that they didn't want to part with them.

"Well," Mrs. Reilly said, "I have some, but you won't want

218

them." And she produced from a closet some marvelous hats. When I got them back to the dorm, the girls screamed for joy, and Barbie grabbed a big black satin hat with bittersweet orange berries and ancient orange ribbon and said, "This is *mine!*" I took a small Mary Poppins hat that some long-lost lady had made of grey tweed and lavender satin in alternating strips, a flat pancake, and put it on my head. It made me look like a proper governess on a holiday.

But the best one of all was a faded blue straw with wreaths of lavender ostrich feathers dripping and falling from its squashed brim, a dashing hat such as our mothers wore in 1910. This poor but elegant hat had been punched, kicked, and used for a football by a team of little boys, to judge from its decrepitude, yet it managed to retain an air of authority. I put it on and pulled it down on one side. The girls rolled on the floor and yelled and laughed until they cried. The hat made me look like a cross between a member of the British aristocracy and a whore in an old movie about Jack the Ripper. It lived up to the very essence of hatness; it changed me into another woman.

The hats piled up in boxes down in the basement, where I had to keep the door locked, for the girls were going insane over millinery. My sitting room was the intermediate warehouse, and the hats were on the floor, in the chairs, under the furniture; every evening we were tearing them apart and making them over with artificial flowers, ribbons, scarves, and little plastic animals. We gave them names in the best designer tradition. One of my favorites was the "King Kong" hat, which was an innocuous beige felt sailor with a black ribbon and a little black plastic chimpanzee on the front. There was the "Votes for Women" hat, a severe navy blue sailor with a large white plastic narcissus sticking up straight as a dagger in front; the "Snows of Kilimanjaro" hat, a white plush pancake with cobra satin horns and a plastic leopard; the "Eliza Doolittle" hat. We hit the jackpot at the home of Miss Mary Taft, a lady who walked with two canes; ten old boxes from Chicago, Stamford, Boston, New York.

One day Mrs. Littlehale called from the Inn and said in a pained voice, "I have a hat I might give you, but I cannot bear to do it, so I have it sitting on my kitchen drainboard and I am looking at it every day, trying to decide."

"We would love to have it, but you mustn't deprive yourself."

"Well, I know I won't wear it any more, but I do love it so much." She hung up.

A day or two later, I came home and found Mrs. Littlehale's hat all wrapped in white tissue paper. It was the most beautiful old Italian straw I have ever seen, a golden wheat color with a brim, and a ribbon to match, a hat of perfect proportions, the kind that made one remember with nostalgia the days when ladies were ladies and wore such hats with long fragile dresses of thin batiste.

There is nothing like a brim to hide under; and one of the memorable moments in my life was when I got on a train with a beau who was seeing me off. I went with him into my roomette wearing a straw hat with a green velvet ribbon and red cherries on it. He kissed me farewell, and the hat fell backward on the floor; he stayed on the train until after it pulled out. By the time we got to Feather River Canyon he said, "I knew *something* was going to happen as soon as I saw that hat." This was a lovely trip.

Meanwhile, Lisa complained, "My mother has lots of old hats and she wouldn't give me a single one. It makes me so *mad* at her!" And I had visions of my own closet shelves, and the memory of how it took me two years to give away my mother's last hat, which she wore with me to church on her last Easter, a grey straw with a band of velvet pansies and a purple ribbon.

Ted Reilly, who was a selectman, gave us a beloved old hat, so battered and worn from resting on Mr. Reilly's large head for lo, these many years, that it was almost human; the girls were wild for this hat.

Barbie said, "I look like the Big Dump in my hat. Say, when we get all this together, the kids are going to have *hysterics*."

"I hope so," I said. There is nothing for the feminine psyche like some well-planned hysterics. They were very clever to stage one of the wildest scenes in "Hello, Dolly!" in a millinery shop.

220

The hat sale went off without a hitch. Hilary, who lived in another dorm, was chairman of the Hat Committee. She was a monumental girl who should have lived in the time of the Valkyries. The day before the big event, she managed to transport two hundred and fifty-three hats to the gym in a driving rain, and she was drenched. Her bronze hair was shining, her shirt covered with dangling beads, and she had rings on *all* her fingers. She wore pants and suede jackets and was a burnished tan, round, voluptuous, and almost six feet tall. The only word for Hilary was WHOOOOOOM. Her feet were soft-shod and she moved like an Indian.

The boys who were in the hall watched us and carried a few boxes. The sight of Hilary in action was enough to make the hardiest male wonder about the future and dread the success of Woman Unleashed.

As Hilary said of the hat sale, "It was free of frustration." We had big wooden tables supplied by Mr. Rufus, something like the furniture they must have used in the time of *Beowulf,* and the girls covered them with bright crepe paper; also we covered two rows of bleachers the whole length of the gym. It was the most civilized rummage sale imaginable; everyone surged in, including five or six hippie boys, and tried on hats, bought most of them, and didn't haggle over anything.

My best memory of that afternoon is of watching the faces of the girls while they tried on hats before full length mirrors. A woman's face when she tries on a hat is almost indescribable, and when dozens were reflected in big mirrors at the same time, there was a mixture of wonder, questioning, laughter, and serious appraisal that formed in the reflected images a collage of women, each one asking, "Who am I?"

The dean of the college arrived, tall, elegant, in her long tweed coat and grey cap of hair, and tried on hats with a will; she ended by buying my old straw with the cherries around the brim, and hung it in her office, where it provided a note of camp.

Mr. Rufus called up and growled, "I hear you didn't use the tables."

"We did, too. Hilary put them back exactly as we found them—that is why you thought we didn't use them."

"Did you make any money?" Imagine Mr. Rufus asking this! Perhaps he was human after all.

"We made over $100," a respectable sum in 1970.

He grunted and hung up.

In the evening on the way to dinner, I saw the lilac buds showing full on their branches, and the forsythia ready to burst into golden blooms, and felt the air turning toward summer. And in the dorm, everything began to come back into focus. Vive the Mad Hatter. Vanity, gaiety, and charity had never for me been so happily combined.

Friendly Counsel

The time of romping about in spring was over, and we came to the pressing business of choosing senior counselors for the following year; we had to select four to counsel and watch over twenty-four freshmen when they arrived in the fall. There was a serious meeting of the old counselors. Ten girls wanted the job of senior counselor.

"Carol?" Everyone agreed Carol would be fine if she could inhibit her strong tendencies toward being too soft with her friends. Part of being a senior counselor was to set a Good Example.

"Ellen?"

"All she cares about is going out with Phil every night." (Through my mind went the voice of Ellen saying, "I'm trying to find my own man.")

"Artichoke?"

"She would worry too much."

"Vicki?" A resounding "*Yes!*"

The sitting room was foggy with smoke. Tuttle was looking tired. Barbie was rolling everywhere on the floor, thinking with her whole body. Beatrice, who would be the future house president, was listening to her first exposé of a counselor meeting.

"Madeleine?" Absolutely yes. Madeleine was discreet and got her work done, and besides, everyone *liked* her.

We needed one more. "Pat?" Barbie sat up and looked serious. "Pat is too sensitive. She would get terribly upset if any of her girls got into trouble because she is so sympathetic that she takes it all into herself."

"Legs?" Absolutely No. "She is a little girl."

These miniscule summaries of character were so astonishingly accurate that I sat in silence.

The rest of the candidates rated only dismayed expressions and guffaws, so a dark horse came into the running: Melinda.

"She won't do it," everyone chorused. "She said she did not want to apply at all."

But a delegation went down the hall and returned with Mellie, who came in with dignity, her face flushed, tall as a young sapling. For a moment I saw her as she might become, a dignified woman, elegant and full of a quiet authority. But Melinda had not yet settled for elegance, and she sat on the edge of the love seat, wearing her long corduroy pants and navy blue sweater. Her face was alight with the look of someone who has found out she is really wanted and needed.

"Well, if you all feel that way—she said, trembling.

Who can resist knowing that she is wanted by everyone who counts in her world? I saw Mellie's shyness fall away, and she said to me later, "I guess it was a form of snobbishness."

Cambodia and Kent State

Cambodia! In what is sometimes the merry month of May, the foolishness, the childishness of water fights and chocolate pie missiles (and I am obliged to admit, such considerations as raising money for local concerns) were bombed out in a single day. I was caught between my realization that I was coming into the time of life when I was engaged in "the process of subtraction," the better to find inner space to grow in, and the sudden need of the girls to enlarge their small world of self. It was in this important week of May, 1970, when we came to the crunch where I had the most trouble with inner patience.

I was at Richard Eberhart's the evening the news of the "secret bombing" of Cambodia erupted like a poison gas from a smouldering volcano. Perhaps we all remember where we were that night, just as we remember the precise scene around us when President Kennedy was murdered. The lights went out inside; in the case of Cambodia, there were no candles to light.

I had been jolted to awareness, in the long evenings of listening to the harsh, disillusioned poetry the boys were writing, and the compassionate, fine-edged responses of the one girl in the class, of my deep personal concern for the student riots: the wild, extended, enormous temper tantrums rising into violence and bursting from the young intellectuals, radicals, and hangers-on of our most distinguished universities and burning down through layers of colleges, the anarchy of desperation. With regard to this, there was nothing in my experience to remember, except one terrible night in Paris in 1968. Who can recall the late sixties without a mingled sense of anger and nausea, as if a civil war was raging? The trashings, the beatings, the bombings, the cruelty, the hatred—and the fatuous responses.

At Wadleigh, we had not been in personal contact with riots. In retrospect, I see that the emotions of my generation wavered, all too often, between helpless horror and a vicarious, voyeuristic satisfaction over the violence we could not ourselves express. We constructed a rationale and debated the issue of youth in revolt with expertise and a betraying passion. I am referring now to those of us not in the line of battle at Berkeley, Columbia, Harvard, and dozens of other colleges which were quite literally torn apart. Someone has said, "It is fortunate that children are small, because if they were large, they would be dangerous." In all humility, I must say that had I been doused with ink and my office trashed or bombed, I would not have had the fortitude displayed by hundreds of professors who kept their sanity.

Professor Eberhart said, "At nine o'clock, we will stop and listen to a special message from President Kemeny." Dartmouth College had at one time called out the police, and I saw in the boys' faces weariness, disgust, determination, anger, as if they felt very old and tired. Looking at the boys then, I realized they were fortunate to be in a small class, close to a man they respected while they learned to articulate their frustrations. He was benign and firm; he was wise. He saw the boys as "the creative life here," and in the creative life he trusted. There was nothing here to remind one of plastic auditoriums with fluorescent lights and a lecturer at a distance. The old house embraced us, contained our anger.

226

At nine, President Kemeny spoke. "We are releasing all students from classes for one week, and we will place all the facilities of the college at their disposal . . . The question of winning a war bears no real weight with students today, for the sense of humanism felt by most doesn't allow war to be considered as a solution." The apprehension, the fear and sense of betrayal which had been running like ice water along our nerves receded. Betty Eberhart brought cocoa and doughnuts and we talked quietly around the big dining room table, then left.

I thought about Richard Nixon; he was an old story to me after my thirty-five years in California. It would be more correct to say I *felt* an old distrust and a new fury. It is too easy, almost cavalier, to speak of what has been fully documented and portrayed by wiser heads than mine: the small, secretive, frightened man inside a brittle shell that cracked. But to be quite fair, it is doubtful if American voters go to the polls with their brains tuned to a cool precision. Not I. It is at a gut level where a nickname like "Tricky Dick" comes forth from the body politic. His one remark, "You won't have Richard Nixon to kick around any more," on the occasion of his defeat in California, was the measure of the inner man, as an arc can be the measure of a circle. It does not matter that he cried. What matters is that he was having a prophetic moment of truth which would become a reality many years later.

And driving along, feeling troubled, on a quiet country road, I realized that for the past two years I had been living a peculiarly introverted, narcissistic life, preoccupied first by my own conflicts and fears over aging, and next in a Wonderland of my own youth—a weaving back and forth of threads between the past and the present, brought to terms at rare intervals by Victoria, by Preston, by second-hand translations of the news media. It was the old, rutted habit of withdrawing from what was too painful, too unpleasant, the old glossing-over; the mind glibly talking *about* while emotions were getting their "kicks" out of the excitement and energy of revolt, or the "I'm-glad-I'm-here-and-not-there" brand of complacent cowardice.

When I arrived at the dorm, I found the girls sitting in the living room, quiet and stunned, limp, like patients coming out of

227

anesthesia. It was past ten o'clock and there was no noise. I sat down with them. It felt like a Quaker meeting. The telephone went unanswered. Olive, a quiet girl whose older brother had been killed in Vietnam, was crying. The faces were solemn.

Pat looked up. "What is there to believe in? One day some of us went downtown with a petition against the War, and a lady in a nurse's uniform said we were *selfish, affluent* brats."

Ellen: "We are, most of us. Nursing all the way."

Victoria got up on her feet and spoke in a trembling, angry voice. "I *have* to stay disinterested. I had so much of war that I can't bear all the *talk*. Americans *talk* so much and they don't know anything about living in a war."

More silence. Melinda: "We have a loud-mouthed system, Victoria, and if we ever lose it, that will be the day we go down the drain."

The notion of "blooming" into maturity was not true any more. I think they saw at this moment that imagining flowers were mightier than tanks was rubbish. After years of indulgence and lotus-eating, they were grinding their way out of fantasies. Were we, as David Reisman said, witnessing a generation "who were picked up whenever they cried?" Or the generation whose parents came out of World War II wanting to give their children whatever the postwar prosperity provided, and were shocked to discover that some of the children despised material prosperity and the system of values which created "conspicuous consumption."

They were up late that night. They were not intellectual, and they were almost entirely apolitical, reflecting the conservative opinions of families who had brought them to rural New Hampshire to a nice, safe, small campus.

"It's about time," Victoria remarked, "that you read the papers and got interested in the U.S.A. and maybe the world. What are you going to *do* about how you feel?"

There is this curious thing about all moments of vision, which may resemble the epiphany of falling in love or the devastating look into disillusionment: all at once we resolve to change, to grow, to overcome our previous blind inadequacies in a burst of commendable resolve. I have always found either

228

of these states touching in the young, to whom one cannot say what experience will teach them; and a ghastly bore in people old enough to know that the vision is succeeded by hard work and "the eternal vigilance which is the price of liberty." Nor is the liberty to be defined as self-indulgence. What we dreamed of and what we have are seldom the same thing.

The slow, daily effort of becoming part of a family, part of a community, and finally of the Family of Man is neither ecstasy nor shock. We cannot judge how someone else is going to do this. Where is Jerry Rubin now? He has written of his return to the plodding journey toward maturity for himself and for his country. I ached inside, thinking of the time of *my* youth, when experience came along more easily, more slowly, and yet? With more polite lies, more self-deception.

The next morning the campus was electric with activity: workshops, hot political discussions, broadcasting in the quad. Rumblings reached my ears concerning high tensions among the faculty: there were those who could not abandon the academic routine. One anguished faculty member said to me, "They are here to *work*." Other instructors found an opportunity for a "teach-in." (My father used to say that even Jesus knew *when* to teach.)

There was no time during this traumatic week when I made any theories; I was too distraught. But I saw that the students had come together outside the dorms, outside the classes, in a way which was not so before. The bonding was campus-wide; the little divisions of dorms, teams, clubs were, for the time being, erased. Whether they became involved in an active protest movement or not there was no shirking; those who were afraid to miss classes studied more diligently. I saw a concentrated community effort.

"If I get up at six and study, I can make it to that workshop on the history of Vietnam—Bernard Fall—have you ever read him?"

"I have to study all the time—I am so close to not graduating, and if I don't graduate, I won't get a job." This was the voice of the unpopular minority.

Oh, I did not go through this time with a clear mind. The

past had become too long, the gap too wide. Bertrand Russell once said, "All of us born before World War I are optimists," a bright generality which could mean many different things. I was old enough to remember the American counterpart of *la belle epoque,* that period in my memory of childhood when Oregon was sun and rain, green and roses; when Hilda the maid rolled out dough for biscuits, bread, cookies, singing, "School days, school days/ Happy Golden Rule days"; when my parents were gods whom one obeyed, and there were three big brothers; when I often heard that I lived in the greatest country in the world. My first memory of politics consisted of sitting with my chin barely clearing the white linen tablecloth and listening to an argument between my father and my three brothers, subject: the Taft-Wilson election campaign of 1912. I would not remember this had not my father taken me on his knee and showed me a newspaper cartoon—Wilson, thin as a bundle of sticks; Taft, a series of puffed balloons.

Britten's "War Requiem" speaks to me now of the ominous breakdown of culture and civilization as the Old World knew it. In 1917 a service flag with three stars hung in the parlor window; my three brothers were in the armed services. My mother cried over letters from my brother Paul, who had gone to Oxford and then left to fly crackerboxes in the A.E.F. over France. My other two brothers did not go overseas, and I remember one of them arriving on leave early one morning, dressed in khaki and flourishing his revolver. Mother knitted socks, helmets, vests, and I learned "The Marseillaise" in French, and "Over There," "Tipperary," and "It's a Long, Long Trail A-Winding" (significantly, "into the land of my dreams"). Armistice Day was a magnificent, wild celebration outdoing what happened in Cincinnati the night after they won the World Series; it was a New Forever, a world "made safe for democracy."

Nor did World War II deflate our overweening pride. What appalled me as I thought of this war was the former excitement over danger; the cause being just, the country united in a glorious effort to conserve needed supplies and to serve in the U.S.O., the Red Cross, the hospitals. Veterans were heroes. And prosperity followed. But "the glory of war" went out when we

230

dropped the atom bomb—we did not rejoice when the mushroom cloud spread over the dead and maimed. This was a glimpse of the apocalypse.

My mother died in June, 1945. Not long before that she said, "I don't want to read the newspapers any more." I was beginning to understand that kind of weariness.

I took down from the bookcase Selden Rodman's *New Anthology of Modern Poetry* (new in 1938) and turned to Robinson Jeffers, "Shine, Perishing Republic."

> While this America settles in the mould of its vulgarity,
> heavily thickening to empire,
> And protest, only a bubble in the molten mass, pops and
> sighs out, and the mass hardens,
> I sadly remember that the flower fades to make fruit,
> the fruit rots to make earth. . . .

I had been reading this poem occasionally for over thirty years, and it now struck into me like broken glass.

> "But for my children, I would rather have them
> keep their distance from the thickening
> center; corruption
> Never has been compulsory, when the cities lie at
> the monster's feet there are left the
> mountains."

Now our children could not keep their distance from the thickening center—they had jumped right into the middle of "the molten mass." This dirty war had been going on in various phases nearly all of their lives, a permanent grubby backdrop. What had any of us sacrificed? Absolutely nothing, except for the citizens who went into battle (including some college students not exempt from the draft) and the people who lost their sons, husbands, fathers, brothers, or received back the injured, the changed.

Beatrice had been reading *The Great Gatsby*. "The American Dream has to change," she said firmly, her dark eyes looking straight into mine.

It was on May 4 that the riots at Kent State resulted in four students being killed and fifteen wounded by a barrage of bullets from the National Guard. In the long, painful years of Vietnam, with all the war dead on the other side of the Pacific Ocean, nothing had penetrated quite like this. I remembered Pearl Harbor; it is the attack on ourselves that really makes us bleed. And when our own kill our own? Assessing the blame becomes almost academic. I still bleed a little over the student at Kent State who cried, "They're *killing* us!" In no other country do they have our assurances of "equal justice for all . . . equal opportunity for all," *E Pluribus Unum*, spelled out so repeatedly that we have a consequent horror at the split between the promise and the reality.

On May 5 there was a day of mourning, black arm bands and very little talk. The students united in a silent protest line that extended along the Main Street on college property. The town police ordered them to desist and disband. What I remember about this time is that the brashness, the noise, the elaborate defensive tactics—hard rock, yelling, singing, silliness—were absent. They were trying to wake up with a feeling of remorse at oversleeping in an important time, and of being half-awake, half-aware, not part of wider political or even humanistic concerns, perhaps a little smug up here away from all those riots and Baddies.

"I guess the faculty was always telling us to be grown-up and now we are trying—some of them can hardly take it. But they are not penalizing us."

Willie and Phyllis were writing letters to the press. In all my frantic reading of papers shoved under my nose for instant criticism, I had not found such concern for the exact phrase.

"We want to do it all over again until it is exactly right," Willie said, her smooth brow creased in a frown.

The voices came to me in snatches.

"You should *hear* what my father said to me on the telephone!"

Parents wept, phoned, worried, when to tell the truth,

nothing dangerous was going on unless you counted differences of opinion.

"I didn't know *how* Victoria felt until she spoke up."

"Victoria isn't afraid of what other people think."

"Legs, stop taking pieces of the *New York Times*. I am reading it *straight through.*"

The voices were in a different key. They reminded me of the voices of women who have had enough of fripperies and follies and being spoiled darlings and have convened to make bandages for the Red Cross.

They were trying on some new roles; was this play acting? Only in the sense that education is play acting from the time we "play house" to the time when we are old enough to stop trying on this and that—the mock United Nations, the sewing class, the art class, the science lab, the student election, a passion for horses, baseball, creative writing—and choose a permanent pursuit somewhere out in the rough-and-tumble of the outside world.

Those of us who had by 1940 committed ourselves to the education of the young as a life-long vocation, had noticed a curious thing about our work (so obvious that it is banal to mention it); our students were always the same age, year after year, whereas we were older. Without the slow year-by-year progression where the students remained immature and fixed in late adolescence, I would have been unable to comprehend the changeless quality of youth. Swept by fads and furies, they always reflected their current culture, yet at the same time were searching for adults - who were not apologetic, ambivalent, or guilty, and would not, as Les Rosten said, "be bamboozled by adolescent irrationality. . . ."

Bamboozled I was not. Nor was anyone searching for me that week. The students were searching for the support of the administration of the college. I could only hope that this frantic week would have some lasting influence on their sense of political responsibility, on a *human* sense of responsibility. At their age I was not exactly a dynamo of social action; at age eighteen or twenty-one, not everyone is adult.

The searching culminated in a mass meeting where addressing the girls as "Ladies" became obsolete. Several members of the faculty spoke with feeling against the War, and in particular, the failure of trust. One girl rose up against the old order of listening politely and often unresponsively to what their elders had to say.

Her question was addressed to the president, "Don't you *care* about all those people getting killed?" she cried out, with tears running down her cheeks. Irene Claremont de Castillejo has written, "There is nothing so ruthless as a woman with a cause between her teeth."

The students had broken through to me, and by this time I knew why their youth was not my youth, even though their world was closer to me now. It had been a year of overcoming my homesickness for the past and for children who remained children, memories of the young strangers who had been the essence of my working life. My need now was to gather it all together in order to discover how to relate to a wider world where one is aware that experience is never merely personal, but *connects*.

Now as I am writing in 1980, I hear that college students are quieter, more passive, more intent on vocational training than on the humanities, more "political" about making changes. In Hanover, I see Dartmouth boys walking around with Byronic haircuts, and the antics on the Big Green in Hanover assumed once again some rah-rah spirit on the eve of a football game, when the hell-raisers built the biggest bonfire ever. Hundreds of railroad ties were assembled log-cabin style with huge quantities of old lumber and combustibles dumped within.

This kind of flamboyant silliness I find strangely reassuring: the fire contained, the hostilities in control. There is a sense of humor we seem to have lost; a sense of humor is a sense of perspective—not that life is funny, but it is absurd, not consistent. Carlyle said, "Happiness is what we have divided by what we expect."

234

At Wadleigh, wine and cheese parties have supplanted cookies, ice cream, and coffee. The dean of students says to address the girls as "Women." I hope they will become visible women; women who know their own identity even when they are alone in spirit or in fact, women not dependent on seeing themselves as reflections in the mirror of someone else's identity. In wholeness there is more to give and more to receive. I would like to know what the students of 1970 are *doing now*. Current history is always like sitting too close to a movie screen, where what we see is blurred unless we are very near-sighted.

Goodbyes—Tears without Pain

I could feel the goodbyes coming on, the sadness of all permanent departures, the new growth. What had I been doing for the past year? The hat rummage sale, comical though it was, represented my need to get out of inwardness. After a year of discovering melancholy, I had been fortunate enough to encounter a cure; now I was ready to go back to the outside world. A college campus in the late sixties could have been more like a descent into hell, but I had happened on one that protected more than it punished.

Whatever I did, returning to a city was not my idea. And I like surburbia even less than cities. I could do without Mrs. Perley and Mr. Rufus, also the library and infirmary close by, and the "belonging" in Wadleigh where I had been sheltered for this interlude (even if the shelter was uncommonly noisy, often abrasive). I would miss concerts and theatre and the excitements of the city, but I needed "belonging." I felt by now that getting old would require closeness to people more than sophisticated entertainment.

What a predicament! All my life I had needed more solitude than most people would enjoy. I did not like "social life" per se, and if I stayed in New Devon, I would have it, teas and luncheons and worthy causes, all of which I am embarrassed to admit do not attract me as much as the smell of printer's ink. New Devon was and is a very *active* town, a rapidly growing town with social groups, social strata. I am no good at this sort of thing; roles again!

For several months, I had been driving along little roads among small villages; one of these was Perrystown, a small village where I sometimes visited an old friend who was building an ell on her old New England house.

"Would you like to have it?" she said. "It will be an apartment completely independent of the house. Income property."

Yes. And so it was that I was able to observe the building of my next home ten miles south of New Devon. I walked around in the bare frame, smelling sawdust and watching a third-generation mason building my fireplace. I found myself making scaled drawings of cupboards, and arguing with workmen as if I owned the place. The ell was surrounded by woods and lawns with exposures to the east, south, and west. It was absorbing to watch the workmen doing what I was intent on doing with my own life; giving it a new shape which formed in my mind as I watched the painters, exclaimed over the old random floor boards a Finnish carpenter found in his barn, ordered plain white muslin cafe curtains for the "nine over six" windows.

I could now approach with equanimity the process of subtraction, which is as natural to age as addition is to the young. I do not mean to imply that this is easy. We do not give up our former energies and all those possessions without a fight. "You are shrinking," my doctor said the last time I saw him, and it was a physical fact; I am an inch shorter. Not to labor the point, one must, like Alice, grow smaller, at least symbolically, or require more assistance to keep up the old establishment.

I need not move into rooms too filled with past essences, nor yet into rooms too brash, too impersonal, or poorly constructed. By June, the apartment would be finished, forty-two by seventeen feet, containing three rooms with shining old boards and white curtains, nothing else except what I chose to take with me. The outside conformed to the old house so unobtrusively that one's sense of proportion was not violated. The inside gave me something I had always wanted, a studio and a home combined. And much later on, I became part of Perrystown, a little village which makes no social distinctions about age and does not blink at eccentricities.

After the revelations of the week we will always call "Cambodia and Kent State," the students were plunged into distraught studying for exams and a month of farewells. Some managed to make it to the protest march in Washington; Rae returned from this with her need "to belong" a feeling deepened.

I discussed with Tuttle what to buy for Barbie for end-of-the-year present, and after solemnly considering a new robe or a dictionary, we decided upon the soft white Snoopy dog from the Village Gift Shop.

"Barbie has wanted that all year," Tuttle said. I didn't blame Barbie; every time I visited the Village Gift Shop, I reached up to feel the Snoopy dog. It was more seductive than a white mink jacket. We had one girl who came to meals clutching an old, bedraggled red fox fur with beady amber eyes. The fox lay on the table while she ate. Barbie would never become this sad, youthful version of Katherine Mansfield's "Miss Brill."

I would not know what happened when Lisa married Larry and Virgie married Jake and Tuttle married Mike O'Connor. There were forty-nine stories I wanted to follow. What happened to Britt, to Helen Todd, who went home early in the year, and was married and had a baby? At least I knew that many of the girls had been accepted in good colleges and universities.

Somehow it was not hard to imagine what would happen to Barbie. But life is an unexpected happening all around. What would happen to me? I didn't know that either, but I felt ready now to imagine I would live to be eighty. And I was ready to leave the dorm; it could not be for me more than an interlude, a retreat which had served its purpose. I could not force time to

238

stop, nor did I wish to; I was ready for life in Perrystown where I was going. There would be new encounters; I looked forward to having neighbors again, and my own place where I could entertain my old friends. The past year now took on the concentrated experience of a prolonged journey, and of returning to have all this added to memory. There was a sense of the past joining with the future.

In May the unfolding came. In one week, the hills turned to masses of pale green velvet, with the staunch evergreens winding their darker shades among the pastures and the frothing birches. The curving drive in front of the dorm was shaded by the branches of old trees, which reached out to touch each other in green arches as they did last summer when I came.

I was learning the old secrets told to me by the people who had lived here for a very long time. I learned where there was a ramshackle hotel with red-checked tablecloths, good drinks, home-made brown bread and crunchy warm pies. This was a place I never found by myself.

I learned where the tall, fragrant narcissus grew in the woods beside a pond, and the wild violets, the trillium with its three-pointed designs repeated in green, mauve, pink, from leaf to center; all these grew where the fresh waters of spring were flowing, released from winter ice to give life to new growing things.

These were the secrets people were beginning to tell me, the things they did not show to those newly arrived nor to transients. To learn these things, I had to wait.

To live with the young was to learn other secrets that we knew when we were young, but some of us have very short memories, or else to remember everything would be unbearable, so we remember only what was good. One of these secrets is that saying goodbye to the past is natural to youth. They cry, sometimes, for every new step in life when we must part with what was familiar makes us cry, sometimes with dry tears. But it is human to want to go on. Nature tells the young that if they settle for a sheltering love, they will not grow. Where they are now is where we are now, in the sense that life and growth mean harder and harder tasks; some day they might look back on their youth as a free time.

Only a few of them would ever be free enough again to run in the rain or make angels in the snow, or scream out every disappointment into sympathetic ears.

And I wondered how old they would be when they did not go off and leave two English bicycles out on the lawn, nine coats in the hall, extra pillows and blankets to be scooped up and given to charity?

I resisted this goodbye. Being a parent, a teacher, a house mother, came to the same thing in the end, a familiarity with farewells in the springtime. On a campus and in every class-room of the world, we said goodbye to those who were ready to go, and they said goodbye to us, and we all reacted with reluctance.

So the State of Euphoria, which was permanently disrupted by the acceleration of the War, was now trembling with the more conventional anticipation of our farewells. To work at the exact point where childhood and maturity meet was to intensify the sensation of letting go. On my sixty-first birthday in August, I had felt a strange, irrational knowledge that said, "Get ready for what you fear." For we put off during all our healthy lives the final lesson, letting go for good and making ready for our own final exams. The young would judge us in the same way that we judged them, when we refused to learn and spent our time jogging up and down in the same spot.

This was the time of rehearsals, and we had the first marching rehearsal for graduation; this took place one evening before the arts center in the gold-washed late rays of the sun.

In the steady, fresh light of morning, it seemed to me the dorm had never looked more dirty and unkempt. Tempers were frayed. Tuttle came in at evening and sat on the love seat with her long nightgown pulled over her knees and tucked under her feet. She said it helped to be in love. She felt kindly toward everyone.

240

"April and Artichoke are being cruel to Piss," she said. "They giggle and talk behind their hands when she comes in. I hate to see people hurting other people."

But this was how some people severed their old bonds. There was more petty "borrowing" now also. We were now in the season of rebellious impulses in strange contrast to the glorious light and air. Barbie went off alone to the ceramics lab; she was tired of her heavy responsibilities, and I was tired of mine. Everyone was tired of the long haul.

I understood now why a family can become so tiresome. Lisa's voice became unbearable, with its nasal clacking; Buffy's hesitant, shy requests seemed louder, and were followed by a silence that meant she wanted something, but whatever was it? I saw Virgie stretched on the couch in an attitude of morose acceptance, becoming the picture of what I feared, loneliness and brooding—so incongruous in Virgie, who at other times was ecstatic when Jake arrived and yelled, "Come on, baby!"

This was also the time when the thoroughbreds did not drop out of the race, and one morning I saw Maria, who had been up all night typing out a project, sitting on the floor of the living room neatly dressed in a white shirt and navy blue skirt, stapling her paper together. Every morning I found some long distance runner on the living room couch, heavy with sleep, finishing an all-night bout of work. The moaners were moaning constantly, and the workers were working with indefatigable zeal. I must confess I found all this studying in spring a violation of nature! The closets smelled musty from winter, and I put moth balls into boxes with the old clothes that seemed to hold in their creases all that was past and gone.

"I wish we could sleep outdoors," Lisa said, "and hear the flag flapping and slapping—it is like being out on the water with spanking sails to listen to the flag on a breezy night."

I laughed. "Can you imagine six hundred girls out asleep on the lawn with the campus police trying to protect them?"

"Oh, that's silly."

One last bizarre incident occurred. At two in the morning I heard a man's voice in the hall; this sound required me to get up and see who was here in the middle of the night. It was the night

241

watchman, Homer, the roly-poly one. He came to my door when I opened it. He told me that a girl in Canby dorm had stuck her hand into the Coke machine in an attempt to make it give birth to a bottle, and her hand was grabbed by the machine. "Miss Barnes was terrific," he said.

"It took us three hours to get her hand out. We had three doctors there, and she was crying, and finally we had to call the garage and have them bring an acetylene torch and *cut* the machine. And the Coke machine man came and said that if anyone had put money in it, it would have cut her hand right off." Homer was still sweating at the memory.

This tale gave me nightmares for the rest of the night. It was the truest science fiction story I have heard. I had visions of someone sticking her hand in a computer; or were computers inviolate brains?

The next day at dinner Mary Barnes told us the story with drama and good humor. All of this mixture composed of foolhardiness, tenderness, childishness strengthened my feeling about leaving. An invisible clock within me was striking the hour.

Exams were beginning, and the girls were packing their trunks, which were delivered from some remote storage room where they had been hibernating all winter. I saw Victoria in an African shirt walking across the campus carrying her first dandelion as if it were a precious flower, a tiny sun.

All the freshmen finished their exams and packed up and went home. The seniors went also, but they would return in a week for graduation, along with the freshmen who would help with the ceremonies. These departures meant that the front hall was full of piles of luggage, bedding, furniture, records, cloth pets, and so much of what appeared to be junk that the parents wailed, puffed up and down stairs, and stuffed things into their cars and station wagons until every vehicle resembled a moving van overloaded and bursting. It was an old movie in reverse.

No sooner had one girl got her things together, hugged us all, screamed, "Goodbye," but what another one started. It was reminiscent of the scene last September, except that all shyness and fear was gone. The parents looked as if they were rearing elephant children and gave forth heavy sighs. Some of them seemed afraid that their peace at home was about to go up in exploding rockets.

Some cars would not contain the belongings, which were tied on roofs and stuck out of windows. The whole back campus was covered with parked cars, and everywhere as far as the eye could see, they were being loaded up. But finally it was over, and the evening light came down softly, with its message of rest. The big house was empty, but I did not feel lonely. With the afternoon sun going down and the trees flooding with green, it was a grateful time. The whole year seemed to have squeezed shut like a tired accordion, with nothing more to play except "Pomp and Circumstance." Silence had never been more beautiful. Taking care of myself and moving to my new home seemed an easy task.

In my week alone, time opened out again the way it was before we made up clocks and calendars—it flowed continuously like water that is not interrupted. I heard the carillon, which was the only sound to mark the hours, and the green campus stretched out as if resting from the feet traveling over it so urgently. Dandelions dotted it everywhere, and the grass was now a thick, soft carpet.

It was the kind of time when one could not say *No* to anything, for everything was saying *Yes, Yes, Yes,* like Molly Bloom. It was the season of burgeoning lilacs, fragrant new-mown grass, light breezes lifting pale fresh leaves.

Were the seniors ready to leave? They would find in the university, in the job in an office or hospital, or in the apartment in a big city, no further protection from the outside world; they would begin the task of creating their own worlds. I had fears for some; I had a feeling that Lisa was not ready for marriage, but Tuttle and Virgie were perhaps on the winning side. The slangy saying, "You win some and you lose some," was appropriate. How could I know when Chace would find her own world? Of Ellen I had no doubts. But almost everyone had taken a step, had learned not to be homesick, had been forced to work, had given something to someone else. There had never been a June in my years of teaching when I did not agonize over a few F's. It was the old lesson; where they were going, I could not go.

And was I ready? Yes. The trauma of my own children's departure into the world was over and healed; I would no longer brood over the past. Not once in this year so brimming with youth had I received so much as a hint that I was an "old lady." To accept the future now seemed to have some advantages connected with an inner freedom, simple things like making my own routine, sleeping with only the sounds of owls and crickets, time to think, time to gather up my life, a slower tempo, a richer remembrance, a freedom to choose—a final conviction of usefulness. It was no small thing—and all the despair of the previous summer seemed now a self-indulgence, a fantasy. I would not be cheerful always; it was not my nature, but I had a new sense of reality.

It was a sunny, crisp day for Baccalaureate, and on the quad we had an immense tent in the shape of a T, with green garlands wrapping all the posts that supported it, and thin plastic curtains swinging down the sides. From inside the tent, the campus looked like a Renoir painting, green watered light, radiant color.

The metamorphosis took place as it does at all celebrations, at all times of rejoicing; the girls got up and went to the senior breakfast dressed in colors like the wet wings of butterflies.

In the air I felt the peculiar ambiance of concentration, a different kind of concentration from the tight misery of exam week. The nature of permanent goodbyes demanded that we unite before we scattered to faraway places, never to be all together again.

Some time after the commencement ceremonies, when there was a great rush to leave, a traditional taking of pictures and a hectic confusion in the old house with all its doors and windows open, I saw an envelope on the bulletin board addressed to me.

I took the envelope down and stood in the hall to open it. There was a card in black and white, with a clownish, smiling little figure on the front, a figure drawn by a child from the International Child Art Center in San Francisco. Inside the card was a handwritten message with a quote from Kahlil Gibran. Why is Kahlil Gibran so popular with the young? I wondered. What was touching was that someone wanted to share her feelings.

"When you part from your friend, you grieve not;

For that which you love most may be clearer in his absence, as the mountain to the climber is clearer from the plain."

The card was from Les, from Little Myrtle, dear, messy Les, who sat sulking in her bare room the day she came with her purple hat on, and would not speak to her father. Les who spilled tea on a twenty-dollar art history book, who became a child last Hallowe'en, then a big sister to Lisa. Les said, as I read on, my eyes clouded by tears I had not thought would start, "I am going to miss you deeply. What you have taught me just by living with us I will always carry with me . . . "

Then I called, I ran down the corridor, and Les appeared, looking very shy, and I took her in my arms, breaking all the rules I had made for myself about goodbyes, and Les and I cried the tears that have no pain in them. It was the moment of a true meeting. For what they taught me was more than what I taught them; it had been a true learning, for we did not know we were doing it at all.

One cannot say, "You have given me back my life."

I left then with a sense of peace. In this year I remembered my own youth and it came together with my own age.